D1563789

STRATEGIC PLANNING

STRATEGIC PLANNING

How to deliver maximum value through effective business strategy

Robert G Wittmann
& Matthias P Reuter

KOGAN
PAGE

London and Philadelphia

Publisher's note

Every possible effort has been made to ensure that the information contained in this book is accurate at the time of going to press, and the publishers and authors cannot accept responsibility for any errors or omissions, however caused. No responsibility for loss or damage occasioned to any person acting, or refraining from action, as a result of the material in this publication can be accepted by the editor, the publisher or any of the authors.

First published as *Unternehmensstrategie und Businessplan. Eine Einführung.* by Robert G Wittmann (Hrsg.), Alexander Littwin, Matthias Reuter, Gerhard Sammer.

First published in Great Britain and the United States in 2008 by Kogan Page Limited

120 Pentonville Road
London N1 9JN
United Kingdom
www.koganpage.com

525 South 4th Street, #241
Philadelphia PA 19147
USA

© 2004 by REDLINE WIRTSCHAFT, REDLINE GmbH, Heidelberg, Germany. A sister company of Süddeutscher Verlag | Mediengruppe. www.redline-wirtschaft.de. All rights reserved.
© Kogan Page, 2008

The right of Robert G Wittmann and Matthias P Reuter to be identified as the author of this work has been asserted by them in accordance with the Copyright, Designs and Patents Act 1988.

ISBN 978 0 7494 5233 9

British Library Cataloguing-in-Publication Data

A CIP record for this book is available from the British Library.

Library of Congress Cataloging-in-Publication Data

Wittmann, Robert G
  Strategic planning : how to deliver maximum value through effective business strategy / Robert G Wittmann and Matthias P Reuter.
    p.   cm.
  Includes index.
  ISBN 978–0–7494–5233–9
  1.   Strategic planning--Handbooks, manuals, etc. 2.   Business planning--Handbooks, manuals, etc.   I. Reuter, Matthias P.   II. Title.
  HD30.28.W597 2008
  658.4'012--dc22
                              2007048612

Typeset by Saxon Graphics Ltd, Derby
Printed and bound in India by Replika Press Pvt Ltd

Contents

List of Figures

Preface

When business people develop strategies, they are confronted by challenges on different levels. They must convince customers to accept their offer through competitive solutions. They need to build enthusiasm for their corporate goals throughout the corporate team. They enter into profitable partnerships. They must convince both investors and organizational management of their business model. Only those who manage to recognize all the opportunities in their corporate environment, those who can realize outstanding ideas as successful concepts and put them into practice effectively and flexibly, can lead their organization on to lasting success.

The idea for this book was conceived against the background of these challenges in connection with a number of consulting projects undertaken by the authors. Both entrepreneurs and their teams have repeatedly demanded an integrated, easy to remember procedure for defining value creation strategies and the requisite measurements to realize them.

This book is intended to assist:

- business people who need to reorient an existing business in a new competitive environment;

- successors of entrepreneurs who need to develop and implement strategies to ensure the continued success of an existing business;

- executives with corporate responsibility ('intrapreneurs') who are responsible for developing their business unit strategically and operationally;

- innovators and their teams who drive products, process and market innovations in a young, developing organization;

- collaboration partners who identify and develop synergies in the value creation chain through systematic collaboration;

- consultants who support entrepreneurs and their teams in value oriented business development;

- investors who analyse business concepts for their intrinsic value on the basis of strategy oriented enquiries.

Each chapter contains central questions, instruments, workshops, practical tips and suggestions for further reading. This outline enables the reader to:

- focus on all the relevant elements of the strategy related to the central questions;

- apply the strategic management instruments that are demonstrated in a coherent strategy with clearly recognizable competitive advantages;

- develop the basis for business plans in the workshops;

- successfully apply the practical tips;

- increase knowledge of the various aspects of strategy indicated in the chapter through further reading material.

In order to simplify the transfer of knowledge gained from the strategic key questions and instruments to their application in the reader's own business, each section has a structured workshop with instructions for its implementation. These are meant to be taken as an invitation to develop ideas for sketching out a business plan while working through this book. In addition, the suggested structure can be used by members of a strategy team who will be able to develop a common understanding of the strategy and to formulate this in a business plan. In this book we wish to offer both orientation and practical suggestions to our readers.

The case study in the appendix is an example of how to apply the instruments of strategic planning shown in this book. Special thanks to Alexandra Leimbeck for contributing to this case study.

About the Authors

Professor Robert G Wittmann, born in 1962, is Professor of Innovation Management at Ingolstadt University of Applied Sciences and partner in ADDventure Consulting GmbH. He has been involved in the concept development and implementation of value based strategies in a large number of projects both at home and abroad for international clients such as Audi, Metro, Siemens and Thyssen-Krupp. Professor Wittmann also advises companies during their startup and growth phases and promotes the ongoing creation of an entrepreneurship network along with partners from the worlds of science, business and economic development.

Dr Matthias P Reuter, born in 1974, began his career in visual merchandising, after which he was involved in the launch and development of a marketing consultancy. His focus in economic research is on strategy implementation. As a senior consultant for strategy and finance, he has been responsible for various implementation projects at Siemens in the fields of strategic management, business planning, and mergers and acquisitions. Dr Reuter is currently head of Strategy, Sales and Finance in Siemens AG's Training and Education Division, realizing corporate performance programmes.

List of Abbreviations

AIDA   Attention, interest, desire, action

BA©   Business assets

BSC   Balanced scorecard

BV   Business value

CAPM   Capital asset pricing model

CC   Capital charge

DCF   Discounted cash flow

E   Equity

EVA®   Economic value added

FCF   Free cash flow

R&D   Research and development

D   Debt

DI   Degree of implementation

MVA®   Market value added

MVD   Market value of debt

MVE   Market value of equity

NOPAT   Net operating profit after tax

PESTEL   Political, economic, socio-cultural, technological, environmental, legal

P/M   Product/market

re   Rate of return for equity

rf   Risk free rate of return

rd   Rate of return for debt

rm   Rate of return for the market portfolio

RMS   Relative market share

Tc   Corporate tax rate

TMV   Total market value of the company

SBU   Strategic business unit

USP   Unique selling proposition

WACC   Weighted average cost of capital

1

The Entire Model

An integrated understanding of strategy

KEY QUESTION

What is strategy?

It is enough, to adjudge the opponent correctly, to concentrate one's own strengths and to win the people – that is all.

Sun Tzu

More than 2000 years ago the Chinese warrior-philosopher Sun Tzu wrote a book, *The Art of War*, that even today may well be the world's most valued and influential book on strategy. Sun Tzu describes how victory can be achieved without fighting by using the appropriate strategy.

According to Sun Tzu, this is achieved:

- by understanding the surrounding circumstances and the power of the opponent;

- by establishing overwhelming strength;

- relative to the parties involved: through political dealing, the use of psychology and convincing communication.

Sun Tzu's three aspects still express the essential elements of strategy today. Strategy, a central task of management, is characterized by the following criteria:

- Profit potential. Decisions that determine the basic direction of the business development are strategic. Through these decisions, possible courses of action are realized that lead to future success.

- Value based orientation. This involves a strategy that contains the development, an encouraging vision that provides the path for long-term development and the structure of a set of objectives aimed at generating value creation for all relevant stakeholders.

- Competitive advantage and customer advantage. The goal of this strategy is to guarantee the long-term success and survival of the business. This can only succeed if the business offers its products and services in a manner that is advantageous from the customer's perspective. Such advantages can be fundamentally established and defended through higher quality, higher profit potential for the customer or achieved through the factor of time, such as a more rapid provision of the service. Competitive edge is the platform for the creation of customer advantage.

- Market strategies and resource strategies. A successful strategy must reflect two perspectives. First, the positioning of the business in its environment and, second, the composition of its internal competences.

- Corporate strategy. Strategies may be found at different levels in the business. In strategic planning at the highest management level, the main focus is the general direction of attack for the entire business, in order to achieve growth strategies, and in stabilizing or minimizing strategies. This is based on the opportunities and risks present in the environment and the market.

This is achieved:

- through portfolio management, ie by setting up and structuring independent business units managed in an entrepreneurial manner;

- through a policy of synergy, ie by activating the value creation between the individual business units;

■ through allocation of resources, ie by making personnel, material and financial resources available.

■ Business strategy. This focuses the strategic business units on establishing competitive advantages in a specific market. The question of which opportunities and risks are present in the environment as well as how the strengths and weaknesses of the business are developed or minimized is dealt with.

■ Functional strategy. This business strategy provides a frame of reference for the development of operating plans for the individual functional areas of operations in order to achieve value creation.

■ Systematic thinking. The competitive environment, together with the business and its subordinate systems, forms a complex system connected by a wide range of interdependent relationships. Strategists must thus meet the challenge of:

– recognizing, understanding and giving form to the interdependent relationships between the parts of the system (systematic);

– working with the developments in the system (dynamics) and configuring them proactively;

– establishing controlling tools that guarantee the long-term survival of the business (learning).

In an era of highly complex, networked structures and processes, it is essential for a strategist to go beyond the simple linear approach. The processes of thinking, planning and acting must not only be carried out with an awareness of these networked relationships, it must also make use of them. This is, in reality, more easily said than done. Many mistakes are just waiting to be made when dealing with complex systems. The key to success is to avoid making them.

Which principles can be applied to avoid these cardinal sins in strategy? As these are a threat to the very existence of the business, the question arises as to which principles can be applied to prevent them. This is where the art of strategic thinking, a process based on the observation of natural laws, comes into play. There are eight rules that

Strategic mistake	Description
Wrong goal description	Instead of pursuing long-term corporate survival and sustainable yield, short-term, isolated problems are declared to be the objective. This planning occurs without any direction, rather like a beginner playing chess.
Non-systematic analysis of the situation	The dynamics of the system, eg the feedback of the situation loops between the various elements in the system, are not taken into consideration. Instead, vast quantities of data are gathered, yet fail to provide an overview of the situation.
Irreversible focus points	The first correctly recognized focus point is declared a favourite. Because of initial successes, other more important tasks are no longer taken into consideration or are even rejected.
Unnoticed side effects	Trapped in the linear cause/effect philosophy, much energy is expended on aiming for the goal and applying measures that appear to be appropriate in order to improve the situation. No tests are conducted to determine the effects on other subsystems and the repercussions for your own business.
Tendency to over-manage	The long-term effects of changes made in the system are undervalued. The resulting massive intervention can destroy the system entirely.
Tendency to authoritarian behaviour	The power to change the system, together with the belief that one has understood the strategically networked elements involved, leads to blind, authoritarian behaviour, which puts the sustainability of any developments at risk.

determine the criterion of survivability. By following them, it is possible to avoid the worst errors in planning. They can also be used as a checklist for determining a successful strategy.

Survival principle	Description	Relevance to strategy (example)
Principle of independence from the product	Strategies are to be function oriented and not product oriented. Products come and go. Functions, however, remain.	• Derivation of competitive advantages from the functions that customers expect
Principle of feedback	In a dynamic environment, feedback loops on the effectiveness of the strategy are mandatory for success.	• Setting up a process of implementation with phases, analysis, conception, application and controlling • Setting up the feedback of key stakeholders in the business
Principle of independence from growth	Because there is no such thing as endless growth, the survival of the business is also to be assured during periods of equilibrium.	• Search for qualitative competitive advantages • Creation of an innovative climate • Setting up a learning organization
Ju-jitsu principle	Strategies employ existing, even troublesome forces, in accordance with the principle of Asian self-defence. This means, in contrast to boxing, using the opponent's strength to one's own advantage.	• Analysis of trends in the environment • Taking the expectations of the stakeholders into account
Principle of multiple uses	Products, functions and organizational structures in a business should be used in many ways.	• Know-how transfer • Information management • Platform strategies • Synergy management
Principle of cycles	Resources are reintegrated into the system through cycles.	• Modularity in products and processes • Reduction of complexity
Principle of symbiosis	Variety in the system and the exchange of complementary competencies permit an innovative survival strategy.	• Cooperation instead of competition • Strategic alliances
Principle of biological design	Products, processes and structures should be oriented to human biological requirements.	• Communication • Orienting the corporate culture to the needs of stakeholders

Survival principles adapted from Vester and applied to strategy.

Method

The manifold aspects of the term 'strategy' are consolidated in Figure 1.1. The key to successful strategies involves three levels.

Level 1: Business value

A leadership philosophy based on the principles of value orientation is the central point. The objective is to increase the business value in the long term and to guarantee the continuing satisfaction and enthusiasm of investors and other stakeholders. The demand for this management concept has expanded considerably in recent years. When only the shareholder approach is followed, this leads to a one-dimensional understanding of value orientation in the sense of shareholder value. Value oriented management in the wider sense requires the consideration of all

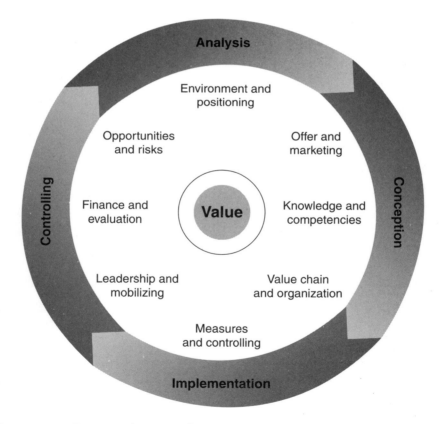

Figure 1.1   Creative fields of the strategy

stakeholders who have an impact on the competitive playing field. Together with the investors, there are the customers, suppliers, competitors, partners, employees, management, government and society to focus on. Success for the stakeholders can be achieved through the distribution of the proper percentage of value through the strategic and operative business model. Value orientation as the overriding vision of entrepreneurial activity is therefore in the best interests of all concerned.

Those who wish to be successful in the long term need to recognize all the opportunities and risks that present themselves in the areas of the stakeholders' influence and to implement them by way of a creative strategy. An orientation exclusively towards value oriented indices at the highest level does not permit the development of businesses towards an objective. Setting up a value controlling and management system that combines value oriented goals with financial or operative value drivers is essential. Thus it is possible to make the requirements for long-term value growth transparent. Experience has shown a definite gap in the implementation of this process. Not all businesses are able to match the business value with the drivers of success. This challenge will be reviewed in level 2.

Level 2: Business model

An action programme based on the requirements of the stakeholders is defined at level 2. The following eight conceptual fields need to be set up and maintained in order to achieve long-term competitive edge: environment and positioning, offer and marketing, knowledge and competences, value chain and organization, measures and controlling, leadership and mobilization, finance and evaluation, and opportunities and risks. A structured consideration of the individual conceptual areas, as seen above, together with a focus on the conclusiveness of the entire concept is of fundamental importance for a harmonious strategic concept.

The development and implementation of a well-rounded strategy requires that the ideas and suggestions be exchanged in a continuous feedback cycle between the stakeholders in the environment. These need to be continuously improved and adapted to meet new situations. This will be reviewed in level 3.

Level 3: Implementation process

A strategic concept can only realize its potential for value creation when it is applied in harmony with the strategic line of attack. In reality, despite vows of commitment to business value and the development of a convincing programme of action, there is an evident disparity in implementation because the entire management process is not followed through accordingly. To realize the implementation, an iterative cycling through the four phases of analysis, conception, implementation and controlling is required. The development and implementation of the strategy is thus guided by a management process. This process examines the factors of opportunity, risk, strengths and weaknesses in order to create a programme to deal strategically, implement the programme consistently and provide quantifiable indices of the path to success. The strategy process thus becomes a feedback cycle in which the requirements of strategically networked thinking can be anchored.

Workshop

Strategy generates a creative tension between a picture of the future of the business and the current situation. Work on this tension in the workshop. Answer the questions given in Figure 1.2 either individually or as a team. This will provide you with the first tools for developing a strategy.

Workshop Picturing the future	
Where is the business today?	Where will the business be in five years?

Figure 1.2   Workshop: Picturing the future

Tip

When you develop a picture of the future, it is helpful to see your business impartially and with an outsider's perspective. Consider the viewpoints of the customers, suppliers, competitors, employees and investors. Which aspects arouse your enthusiasm? Which aspects appeal to you personally?

2

Value Based Management
Creating a successful organization

KEY QUESTION

Is the team focused on a vision that builds enthusiasm?

The superior strategy finds its effectiveness in the interaction of the forces involved.

(Sun Tzu)

Developing an inspiring vision is generally considered to be the best way to win over people to demanding goals in the long term. The vision is an attractive view of the future reality of the business. In the same manner as a compass (Figure 2.1), it can contribute to setting the direction for value oriented business development as well as creating coherency among executives and employees. In this way, visions become an effective means of motivation and a leadership tool that is a guideline for the strategy. This improves and provides self-correction for the use of internal resources and creates a platform for entrepreneurial thought and action. The secret of successful visions lies in formulating them so that they provide an incentive, are plausible, coherent, relevant to the entire business and prove authentic in everyday business life.

Method

A business vision describes comprehensively how the corporate future will appear. There is a wide spectrum of applicable topics here, from the material aspects (eg taking an outstanding position in the area of technology leadership) to the non-tangible aspects (eg living the corporate values). Although each firm's business vision is unique, the following range of topics are frequently found in these visions:

■ aspects of a value oriented self-image (eg 'Make people happy', Walt Disney);

■ advantages that make the business interesting for specific stakeholders, especially customers, employees, partners and investors (eg 'Information at your fingertips', Microsoft);

■ position in the competitive environment relative to the market strategy, the technology and the competences (eg the German phrase 'Vorsprung durch Technik', Audi);

■ present or future organization model (eg 'Global network of innovation', Siemens).

A business vision is effective if it fulfils the following four criteria:

■ Trendsetting – the vision functions as a 'guiding star' by showing a clear direction. It is developed on the basis of a market or industry understanding and shows how to better address customer problems than competitors do.

■ Convincing – the vision addresses positive values, is intuitive and credible. It shows the advantages for the individual organization and generates enthusiasm.

■ Realizable – the vision is challenging but not Utopian. It is, with the necessary effort, capable of being achieved. The executives and the employees are always aware of it. This is part of daily business for everyone.

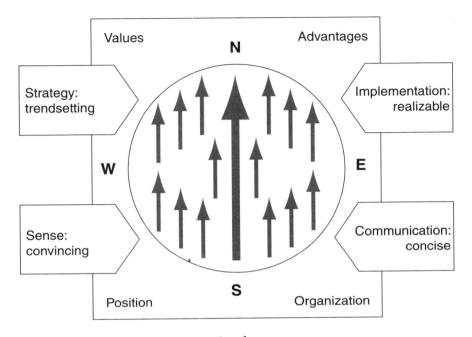

Figure 2.1   Vision as a compass for the strategy
(according to Coenenberg/Salfeld (2003), p.23)

◾ Concise – the vision is easy for everyone to understand, it captures
the message in just a few words and is formulated in an attractive
and distinct manner.

Workshop

Visions often arise from the personal inspirations of the entrepreneurs themselves. A tremendous opportunity presents itself when a team 'unwraps' a vision. The perspective of the future is, in this way, more varied. Frequently, a visionary force arises in the team and supports successful implementation.

Workshop Vision			
Values What are we proud of? What would we really like?	**Advantages** What makes our partners enthusiastic?	**Position** What gives us a competitive edge?	**Organization** What makes us unique?

Figure 2.2   Workshop: Vision

Tip

To achieve a convincing vision in the team, it is possible to conduct an imaginary trip that leads you through the future of the business. The participants are guided by the questions listed in Figure 2.2 to speak of the future of the business as if it were already reality. Such a journey requires a framework in which the participants feel good, and both creativity and intuition are possible. In this process, metaphors (eg sailing ships, gardens, springs, cathedrals, jewels) are helpful for visually demonstrating the uniqueness of the vision.

Take the vision into consideration once again following the creativity phase. Is it in accordance with the criteria: trendsetting, convincing, realizable and concise?

KEY QUESTION

How is the business value realized for the stakeholders?

That which motivates is profit.

(Sun Tzu)

Businesses are in a continuous process of exchange with a range of stakeholders. These groups of stakeholders are composed of customers, suppliers, employees, executives, external investors, shareholders and the government. Each of them expects a specific value from the business. To the extent that the business demonstrates through innovative strategies that the expected value is sustainable over the long term, these stakeholder groups have an enduring interest in successful business development. The provision of capital is, in this sense, the financial basis for the ability of the business to satisfy the interest of each group of stakeholders. In recent years, the interests of outside investors have particularly come to be the focal point of the objective-setting systems of businesses. The reasons for this lie in the globalization of capital markets, the increasing intensity of competition for internationally mobile equity capital and the growing influence of institutional investors. The increase in the value of the company has thus become the cardinal monetary target index. Against this background, the goal of value creation has become the benchmark for strategies and their application. In this context, it is of central importance that the levers of value creation be identified, placed in a consistent strategy and applied resolutely.

Method

In recent years, diverse concepts for value based management have been developed. All of them have in common that they focus on the development of the value of the equity, known as shareholder value. The instrument of economic value added (EVA®) from Stern and Stewart is typical – it is used as the value based management concept in many businesses.

Stern and Stewart have listed the following common problem zones of financial management systems:

■ Businesses often make use of a wide range of different financial benchmarks and methods when, for instance, strategies are evaluated, objectives are set, investments evaluated and financial incentive systems for managers need to be set up. This leads to conflicts in objectives and to confusion and is discouraging for executives.

■ The financial standards typically used for controlling come from the accounting data sources. These, however, are distorted through the weighting applied and stand, at least partially, in no direct relationship to the drivers relevant for the value creation for shareholders.

■ Financial goals are not derived from the expectations of the market, rather, in connection with the budget planning. This causes the managers to undervalue or overvalue the true current potential of their strategies. The motivation and bonus systems for managers are frequently not keyed to the goal of value creation and therefore do not adequately mirror the entrepreneurial opportunities and risks.

Stern and Stewart's concept is aimed at overcoming these problems and setting up a financial management system that optimizes the business value for the shareholder (shareholder's wealth).

Initially, the market value of the business is considered. This is the market value added (MVA®). It is the difference between the total market value (TMV) and the investment in business assets (BA). The business value is composed of the value of the equity plus the market value of the debt. To this end, the market value of the equity in publicly traded firms is determined by multiplying the share price by the number of shares, the value of the outside capital results from the sum of capital the firm has borrowed. Because the share price reflects the expectations of investors regarding the achievable market value of the business in the future, the MVA® can be interpreted as the created value that results from the strategy above and beyond the committed investments. In the interest of the shareholders, Stern and Stewart recommend that the maximizing of the MVA® be set as the highest strategy goal for managers to strive for.

The application of MVA® as the general basis for management concepts is, however, made difficult by several obstacles. The following aspects are especially problematic:

■ The MVA® can only be directly determined for businesses that are publicly traded. Lacking a share price evaluation, a direct determination of the MVA® is not possible for businesses otherwise incorporated or for the business units of incorporated companies.

■ Share prices are volatile and subject to a variety of capital market influences. The MVA® is, therefore, not stable over time. Thus, it cannot be used as a basis within the framework of a management concept for significant commitments to goals that can be used in the implementation of strategies.

Because a general application of the MVA® is not possible, Stern and Stewart transfer the capital market oriented evaluation to the concept of EVA®. This can be examined in an EVA® driver tree (see Figure 2.3). It may be considered as a periodic allocation value from the difference between the net operating profit after tax (NOPAT) and the costs for the equity and outside capital applied (capital charge).

The concept of NOPAT is based on the profit and loss statement and is adjusted in a sequence of several steps to eliminate the distortion eminent in the financial, tax and evaluation process. Expenses from which income is to be expected in the coming years (eg expenses for research and development) are activated as strategic investments and written off over a pre-defined period of time. The resulting increase in NOPAT in the year of the investment is an incentive for managers not to ignore strategic investments. The NOPAT is derived from the operative results from sales less cost on an after-tax basis.

The business assets encompass investments in the interest bearing capital and are equivalent to the nominal variables which are also the basis for the MVA® calculation.

The capital charge (CC) is equivalent to the minimum rate of return that shareholders and outside capital lenders may expect for the capital invested in the business. This is derived from the formula of weighted average cost of capital (WACC). The cost rate for outside capital is calculated on the basis of the interest rate after tax. The shareholder capital costs are determined relative to the risks of the business and calculated into the equation. The weighting of both capital structures occurs according to the desired capital structure, taking into account the market value of the shareholder capital as well as the value of the borrowed capital.

This concept permits the determination of similar values for future periods for the EVA® within the framework of the evaluation of strategies. Stern and Stewart have demonstrated that the present value of the sum of all future EVAs® is equivalent to the MVA®.

Based on the EVA® drivers tree, three fundamental strategic recommendations for taking action for both business development and for investment and divestiture can be identified:

■ Increasing the operating profit (NOPAT) with the same amount of capital commitment. This can be achieved through programmes to increase sales or through the lowering of operative expenses.

■ Strategic and operative investments in projects with positive EVA® or with a positive present value for the future EVAs®. These projects permit an anticipated return that is higher than the cost of capital.

■ Disinvestments in areas that show a negative EVA® or lead to the expectation of a negative present value for the future EVAs®.

Stern and Stewart show four fields of application (the 'four Ms of EVA®') for their management system:

■ Management (planning and budgeting). The EVA® should be used for the conception of strategies and as an evaluation and measurement tool used as a basis for decisions on the objective of value orientation when committing resources.

■ Measurement (reporting). The EVA® should be the object of both internal and external reporting, since it shows all three of the basic options for increasing the business value.

■ Motivation (compensation for managers). Managers should conduct themselves as entrepreneurs and base their decisions on the same criteria that investors would make use of. The compensation system for managers should therefore be coupled to the EVA®, and the corresponding levers the managers can influence within the EVA® drivers tree should be addressed.

■ Mindset (cultural change). The anchoring of the EVA® as a management variable should effect a change in the business culture toward more entrepreneurial behaviour and value orientation and also support decentralized decision-making processes.

Stern and Stewart suggest a three-phase project design for the implementation of their concept:

■ In phase 1, Readiness, a framework concept based on the EVA® to measure success, should be set up. This is to provide the business management with transparency and to demonstrate the advantages of the EVA® concept.

■ In phase 2, Design, the planning and reporting systems and the compensation system for managers are defined by the EVA®.

■ Phase 3, Implementation, centres on aspects of communication and developing competency. Managers, employees and external stakeholder groups need to be won over to the concept in this phase.

Although the Stern and Stewart concept places central emphasis on the optimizing of business value for the shareholder, an examination of the EVA® driver tree shows that the strategic process of optimizing can only be successfully carried out in the long term if the interests of the remaining stakeholder groups are adequately taken into consideration. This means that from the perspective of the customer there must always be an advantageous price/performance ratio compared to that of the competition for the offering. Employees and managers need to be provided with the necessary perspectives to fully exploit their competences, develop these further, and as a result be able to generate sustainable competitive edge.

The EVA® driver tree shown in Figure 2.3 can be used as an instrument (EVA® driver analysis) in each phase of the strategy process, from analysis through conception and realization to success review. It can be used to identify and evaluate the value creators (levers). The formulation of these levers as well as an evaluation in the context of the driver

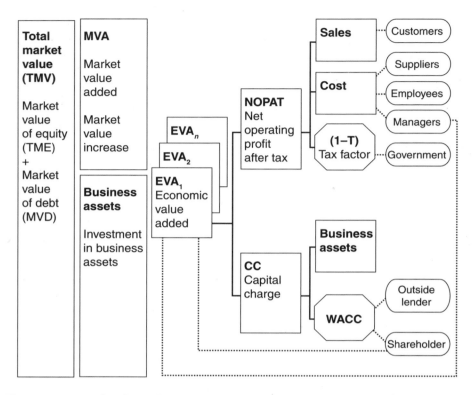

Figure 2.3   Value based management by economic value added (EVA®)
(according to Stewart (1991), p.17)

tree provides the management team with an anchoring point for a common understanding of the essential strategic points of attack and their contribution to the business value. In the table below, possible levers are listed as an example that can be used for the following competitive points of attack. First, using advantageous prices, second, by incorporating superior quality. When conducting an EVA® driver analysis, the type of the business and the specific business situation together with the fundamental strategic direction of attack have to be taken into account.

EVA® driver analysis	Levers for EVA® growth	
	Competition through advantageous prices	**Competition through superior quality**
Sales	• Penetration of the core market by aggressive pricing • Opening new market segments • Developing new markets • Setting up barriers to entry through patent protections and exclusive contracts	• Speeding up the process of innovation • Focus on attractive market segments willing and able to pay • Knowledge of the customer's business model • Differentiation of the offers
Operative expenses	• Tight cost management • Optimizing the production capacity • Realizing advantages for experience • Optimizing the business processes	• Orientation of the range of service to the customer's needs • Platform strategies for reducing expenses • Acquisition of suppliers with excellent quality
Operating assets	• Increasing efficiency • Liquidation of little used assets • Rationalization	• Establish leadership in technology, in production plants and processes
Working capital	• Tight management of accounts receivable • Reduction of inventory • Increasing customer pre-payments	• Directed management of accounts receivable • Adapting conditions • Offer of financing models
Tax rate	• Choice of the legal form of the company	
Cost of capital	• Optimizing capital structure • Reducing business-specific risks by the introduction of a system of risk management	

Workshop

An analysis of the stakeholders provides an initial approach to the concept of value oriented business management. As shown in Figure 2.4, a value for each relevant group of stakeholders is to be created in accordance with the concept of the EVA®. What are the expectations? Which levers can be influenced by using strategies? How is value established for the partner?

Workshop Stakeholder analysis		
Which stakeholder groups are relevant to our business?	What expectations can be identified?	Which levers provide value for partners?
Customers		
Suppliers		
Competitors		
Management		
Employees/Team		
Shareholders		
Outside lenders		
Government		
...		

Figure 2.4   Workshop: Stakeholder analysis

Tip

Because the levers involved in the creation of business value are frequently networked together, it is useful to integrate executives from the various functional areas of the business. In this way, both networked effects and conflicts in objectives can be identified and it is possible to set priorities for application. Furthermore, a clear allocation of responsibilities should be established within the team for the implementation of the identified levers.

3

Environment and Positioning

Identifying opportunities and risks

KEY QUESTION

Which external trends influence future success?

If you do not know the mountains and the forests, the ravines, swamps and moors, you shall not be victorious. He, however, who is victorious because he knows how to change and fit the environment to his needs, deserves to be called a genius.

(Sun Tzu)

In the framework of analysing the macro-economic environment, the factors and systems that may have an effect on the business and its potential are considered. The goal is to include all potentially relevant trends and developments, determine their possible influence and develop the initial strategic courses of action applicable to them. In this context, it is especially important to discover the driving forces that can change the structure of an industry, a market or a specific market segment.

Method

At the beginning of this selection process – in accordance with the PESTEL analysis of Johnson and Scholes – six environmental aspects are to be differentiated: the political, the economic, the socio-cultural, the technological, the natural and the legal. The analysis of the development of the environment should not be a one-off process, it should be anchored as a permanent task in the strategy process. In order to concentrate on the priorities obscured by the large number and interconnectedness of the environmental processes, a classification in both dimensions of probability for the occurrence of the environmental influence and its effect on the business is recommended. Figure 3.1 shows the dimensions of the macro-economic environment using exemplary influence variables.

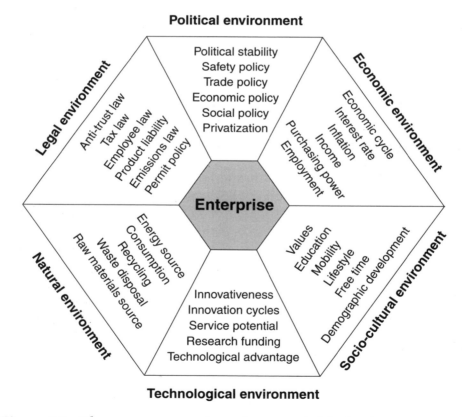

Figure 3.1   The macro-economic environment of the business

(according to Johnson/Scholes (2002), p.102)

Workshop

In the workshop, use Figure 3.2 as follows. The trends for each environmental branch have to be identified first. Building upon this, the opportunities and risks and the probability of the influencing elements occurring, together with the range of their effect on your own business, can be derived. A strategy can then be set up either to effect the rules of engagement in the environment to be influenced (action) or to adapt to the developments in the environment (reaction). The analysis of the action and reaction in the environment and the possibilities of influencing them through your own business indicate the options for strategic action. These are to be made concrete in the conception phase.

To optimize the quality of the analysis, the integration of participants with knowledge of the various dimensions of the environment (if necessary, external experts) and employees from the various functional areas of the business is recommended. A variety of perspectives and insights have a positive impact on the creative potential and the solution-finding competence of the strategy team.

Workshop Analysis of the environment					
Environment	**Trends**				
	What trends are there?	What opportuni-ties/risks are the result?	How great is the probability and influence?	What reactions are there in the environment?	How do we proceed?
Political environment					
Economic environment					
Socio-cultural environment					
Technological environment					
Natural environment					
Legal environment					

Figure 3.2 Workshop: Analysis of the environment

Tip

In conducting an environmental analysis, a variety of sources can be used, many of which are free of charge:

■ publications of international organizations (eg EU, UNO);

■ publications of government agencies at both central and regional level;

■ government statistics services;

■ publications by industry groups and chambers of commerce;

■ business branch reports of lending institutions;

■ market and opinion research institutes;

■ news reports or search engines of media publications (eg business magazines, trade journals);

■ business reports, annual reports, pricing lists, advertising brochures and catalogues from competitors;

■ studies by consultants;

■ databases on the world wide web.

KEY QUESTION

What is the quality of competition in the industry?

Thus it is said: When you know neither yourself nor your opponent, you are in danger in every single battle. When you know both yourself and the opponent, even one hundred battles shall not endanger you.

(Sun Tzu)

The formulation of a strategy consists essentially of placing the business in relation to its competitive environment and establishing sustainable advantages. The structure of each industry has a powerful influence on the rules of the game for the competition as well as for the strategies the business needs to apply. Attention must be paid to the fact that the intensity of the competition arises not only from the behaviour of existing competitors but may additionally be influenced by potential new competitors, existing or suddenly appearing substitutes and the bargaining strength of suppliers and customers. All of these determine the profit potential of a sector and so determine its attractiveness.

Method

The interacting competitive forces and their determinants in the competitive environment can be examined and evaluated using the model for industry attractiveness by Porter. The basis of this tool is an evaluation of the degree of competition among existing rivals. In order to identify strategic groups of competitors, it is helpful to examine similarities in the strategies of existing competitors, paying due attention to the following aspects:

- differentiation of products and services;

- price/service relationship;

- coverage of markets and market segments;

- sales channels used;

- marketing measures;

■ your own value creation;

■ amount of vertical integration;

■ relationship to the key groups;

■ size of the business.

The danger remains, however, that further competitors may enter the sector. The danger of such a market entry is dependent on the height of

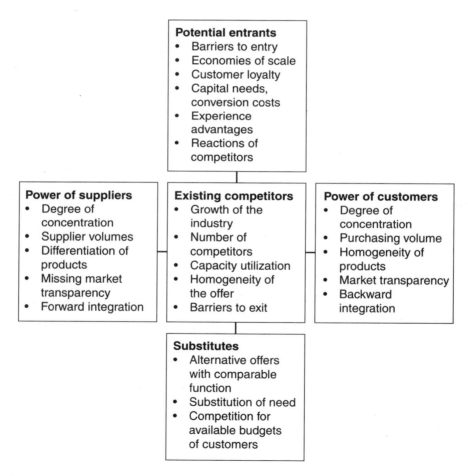

Figure 3.3   Aspects of industry attractiveness

(according to Porter (1983), p.26)

the market entry barriers as well as the reactions that may be expected from the competitors already present. Such reactions might include price wars and product differentiation. The threat potential that substitutes pose must also be taken into consideration. This can limit the rate of return in the sector by setting an upper price limit for the offer. Finally, the bargaining strengths of customers and suppliers need to be taken into account. These can influence the potential rate of return through pressure on prices, quality and willingness to deliver.

Workshop

In the workshop on conducting an industry analysis (using Figure 3.4) the quality of each competitive force is described first. The aspects listed in Figure 3.3 may be used as a checklist for this purpose. To identify the opportunities and risks for the business, you should attempt to estimate the effects resulting from the significant variables. In so doing, you may derive important consequences for the design of the strategy.

Workshop Industry analysis				
Competitive force	What are characteristics of the force?	How does the force develop?	What opportunities and risks are there?	How do we proceed?
Existing competitors				
Potential entrants				
Substitutes				
Power of suppliers				
Power of customers				

Figure 3.4   Workshop: Industry analysis

Tip

In conducting an industry analysis, close attention must be paid to the following points.

The forces in the industry interact with the developments in the macro-economic environment (see PESTEL analysis) and may be influenced by them. The technical development of the internet, for instance, has led to completely new business models and to discontinuities in competition.

The five forces listed are frequently interdependent. Using this, develop a clear case of how changes having an effect on any one of the competitive forces also have an effect on the development of the others.

KEY QUESTION

Which scenarios are possible?

Act after comprehensively reviewing the situation. He who is able to first evaluate which paths are twisted and which straight shall be victorious.

(Sun Tzu)

The success of a chess player is based on the ability to anticipate several moves, if not entire games. When confronting dynamic conditions, not only the past, but also the future and the development of the environment must be taken into consideration. Therefore, an important task of business management is the strategic early recognition of those future opportunities and risks relevant to the environment of the business. The degree of uncertainty increases the further one looks into the future. A means of providing this forecasting with structure and giving it a systematic framework is provided by the scenario approach, which, among other things, is based on the results of the previously conducted environmental analysis and the analysis of branch attractiveness.

Method

The scenario approach is among the best known instruments of strategic early recognition. The objective is to portray alternative future environments as possible consequences of occurrences. The cause/effect relationships and those decision points relevant for the business can thus be identified. Two questions are especially important:

How can the occurrence of a hypothetical situation be broken down into the steps leading to its existence? What alternatives exist in each stage of the process that may be used to prevent a further development or to steer it in the desired direction?

If unanticipated events are excluded, it may be assumed that the near future (two to five years) will be primarily shaped by the status quo (eg today's infrastructure, technologies, patterns of behaviour, legislation). When the distant future (5 to 10 years) is envisaged, it may be assumed that the influence of the current status quo will have an ever lessening effect. In this way, it is possible to picture the expansion of the spectrum

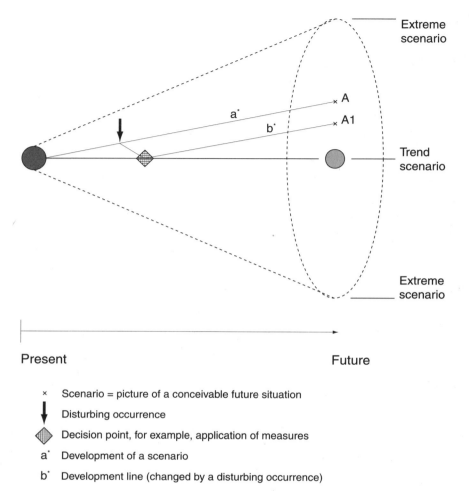

Figure legend:

×   Scenario = picture of a conceivable future situation

↓   Disturbing occurrence

◈   Decision point, for example, application of measures

a˙   Development of a scenario

b˙   Development line (changed by a disturbing occurrence)

Figure 3.5   Scenario cone

(according to Geschka and Hammer (1999), p.468)

of possible future situations as a cone (Figure 3.5). The rim of the cone represents the extreme scenarios, the middle the most probable path, the trend scenario. The effect of possible disturbances may be portrayed through the use of such a cone. If, for instance, the development of scenario A is influenced by a disturbance (arrow), a resulting deviation from the original development occurs that, through the action of the measure (cross-hatch), finally leads to scenario A1. In this model, a 'weak signal' is a disturbance that is registered as a discontinuity that prior to

Steps	Core question and methods
Step 1 **Defining the field to be investigated**	• What is the relevant field to be investigated? (eg business area) • Which structural characteristics and problems determine the field under investigation? (eg products A and B in country Y and Z) • Which descriptors (eg sales) determine the field under investigation, what is their current status?
Step 2 **Identification of the most important areas of influence**	• Which external factors have an influence on the field being investigated (eg price wars among competitors)?
Step 3 **Determining the descriptors**	• Which quantifiable descriptors (eg market volume, market expansion) and qualitative descriptors (eg consumer attitude) characterize the relevant environments? • How are the descriptors developed? • Are the assumptions underlying the critical descriptors consistent?
Step 4 **Creating the scenarios**	• Which bundle of assumptions can be coupled because they are homogeneous, and which are mutually exclusive?
Step 5 **Interpretation of the scenarios**	• How can the scenarios be concisely formulated?
Step 6 **Effects analysis of the significant disturbing occurrences**	• Which disturbing events or discontinuities are conceivable and what influence do they have on the projected scenarios?
Step 7 **Deriving the consequences**	• What response is mandated by the scenarios for the environment under investigation?
Step 8 **Conception of the measures**	• What concrete strategic and operative measures are to be derived and what actions taken? • How can these measures be consistently applied?

the effect on the scenario already makes itself known through such weak signals. This consequently means that reaction strategies are possible before the measure (cross-hatch) becomes possible and thus the development that was to have been the logical consequence of scenario A can still be tracked.

The eight-step process shown on the previous page is useful for applying the scenario approach.

Workshop

In a workshop based on the procedure indicated above, a trend scenario and two extreme scenarios can be derived and the underlying assumptions set (see Figure 3.6). Taking the disturbing occurrences into account, the measures in the next step for the strategy development can be derived. The following methods can be considered.

With this method of brainstorming, all possible ideas, regardless of their obvious applicability to external areas of influence pertaining to the environment being examined, are written down (eg on cue cards).

Next, a process of structuring and cluster building (relative, eg to the interaction and strength of their influence) is carried out using illustrations to facilitate the classification.

Scoring models can be used for evaluating the qualitative descriptors.

Using a standardized questionnaire, the Delphi method can be used to question experts on discontinuities. The experts evaluate which effects are produced by which disturbing occurrences for the selected business target variables. This is achieved by running through every possible combination of result and target variable as a discontinuity. Further, the

Workshop Scenario analysis				
Scenario	How can the scenario be described?	What assumptions are made?	What influence variables and disturbing effects are there?	What measures can we derive?
Trends scenario				
Extreme scenario 1				
Extreme scenario 2				

Figure 3.6   Workshop: Scenario analysis

subject probability of the occurrence of a given event is evaluated. In an evaluation matrix, the most significant discontinuities can be identified and individual disparities can be analysed.

Tip

Practice has shown that for the representation of future developments, one to two scenarios are sufficient. Every time a scenario analysis is done, two contrary extreme scenarios should also be included in order to be certain that: a thorough consideration of opposing developments is possible and not simply a variation from the, as a rule, more easily derived trend scenarios; the margins of the future reality are limited by the extreme scenarios.

The scenario approach requires that one not be limited by 'box' patterns of thinking, but that differing perspectives be considered. A time-honoured approach is to invite outside experts. They formulate opposing hypotheses to the internally generated hypotheses. In this way, it is possible to ascertain that the forecast developments and their influences and the probability of their occurrence are validated.

KEY QUESTION

What are the strengths and weaknesses of the competitors?

Analyse your opponent, so that you may learn his plans, learn from his successful as well as his failed plans.

(Sun Tzu)

Many businesses fail to systematically gather information about their competitors. Instead, they act on the basis of impressions and assumptions. In the final analysis, in order to lead the competition it is of utmost importance to have a profound knowledge of the strengths and weaknesses as well as the behaviour of one's main competitors. It is essential to conduct a detailed competitor analysis in order to carry out a comprehensive strategy formulation.

The objective of a competitor analysis is delineated in three parts:

■ The probable behaviour of each competitor relative to changes in the sector and the expanded environment needs to be determined.

■ The chances for success for the expected strategic steps of competitors need to be evaluated.

■ The potential reactions of competitors to your own possible strategic options should be identified and evaluated.

Based on this analysis, it is possible for the individual business to derive options for its strategic focus.

Method

Porter defined four elements to be taken into consideration for the instrument of competitor analysis:

■ Knowledge of the goals for the future permits a forecast for a pending change in the competitor's strategy.

■ The current strategy of competitors provides clues to the current direction of the competition and to which measures they are using. It is additionally possible to predict how they will behave in the future.

■ The identification of the assumptions of each competitor is directed toward the paradigms on which the competitor bases its competitive behaviour. Based on these fundamental assumptions, it is also possible to draw conclusions about the future behaviour of this competitor.

■ The abilities of competitors are decisive for their ability to sustain their superior position in a competitive environment. These influence their capability to take strategic steps or to counter such steps by the competition. Additionally, these enable the organization to deal with any changes in the sector or the environment. Such knowledge of the relative strengths and weaknesses of competitors makes it possible for the business to occupy the optimal position in a competitive environment.

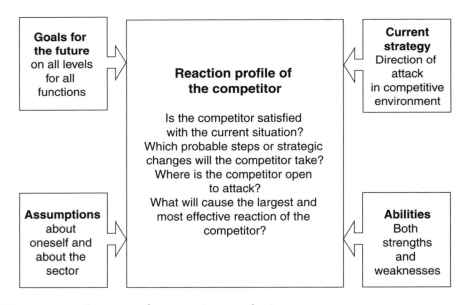

Figure 3.7   Aspects of competitor analysis

(according to Porter (1983), p.26)

Workshop

Prior to performing a competitor analysis (see Figure 3.8), it must first be determined which competitors are to be analysed. In this context, it is important that not only the currently important competitors but also those who are potential competition be taken into consideration.

The goal of the workshop is a synthesis of the four elements described. More comprehensively, a competitor's profile based on the strengths and weaknesses of your own business can be developed that reflects your own competitive strategy.

Workshop Competitor analysis							Plans for the future	Current strategies	Assumptions
Competitor:							Plans for the future	Current strategies	Assumptions
Abilities	What is our position relative to the competitors in question? (Competitor = 0)								How will we proceed?
	+3	+2	+1	−1	−2	−3			
Price/service									
Differentiation									
Market presence									
Sales concept									
Solutions quality									
Financial strength									
Competence									
Innovation strength									
...									

Figure 3.8   Workshop: Competitor analysis

Tip

Gathering knowledge and information about competitors is a challenge that cannot always be mastered by the business on its own. It makes sense, therefore, to make use of external information brokers for this information. Because such services are sometimes extremely expensive, it is best to first process and evaluate all the available information before engaging these services. Highly valuable information can also be gained from employees who have left a competitor and now work in your own business.

KEY QUESTION

How large is the market?

Strategy prefers high places and avoids the plains.

(Sun Tzu)

When making the decision as to whether to enter a new market segment, it is necessary to know the size of the market as well as to determine its development potential both in qualitative and quantifiable terms. The size of the market depends on the number of consumers, their interest in buying, their purchasing power and the access capabilities of your own business. To this end, the following market variables have to be differentiated:

■ Market potential. Market potential denotes the potential capacity of a market for a specific product or service. It is determined by the number of potential consumers, the intensity of the need, the market transparency and the marketing policy measures of the tenderers in the market. Markets that are growing strongly promise large growth rates in terms of sales because of the unused market potential. Generally speaking, relations between competitors in such markets are relatively harmonious. In saturated markets, however, there is usually aggressive competition, since the market can only yield limited growth rates and since any sales increase brought about by a penetration strategy will be at the cost of the competitor's market share. The market potential is useful as an orientation variable for determining the saturation margin and also the market volume.

■ Market volume. The market volume describes the real sales of all those tendering a product or service type in a given period in a specific market segment. This is the portion of the market potential that is achieved by the entire sector.

■ Sales potential. The sales potential is analogue to market potential and is limited to one specific business. It specifies the maximum share of market potential the business can attain. This variable is influenced by the marketing activities of the tenderer and by the price/performance ratio in comparison with the competition and its behaviour.

■ Sales volume. The sales volume specifies the total turnover of units sold by the company over a specific period.

■ Market share. The market share of a business is defined as its sales volume in relation to the total market volume in percentage points. The variable of the market share makes a benchmark with other businesses possible, thus indicating your own position in the market.

■ Relative market share (RMS). The RMS is the ratio of your organization's sales volume to the sales volume of your chief competitor. This variable is of particular strategic significance when determining potential unit cost reductions through the factor of acquired experience. In practice, one may assume that the unit cost decreases with increasing output. This means the RMS can be used as an index for your own cost position in comparison to that of a competitor.

Method

An important factor in the quantification of market potential is the accessibility of markets. The model of market cascading can be used as a tool for the analysis and derivation of a strategy for opening markets. On the basis of market potential, one must first determine what share of the

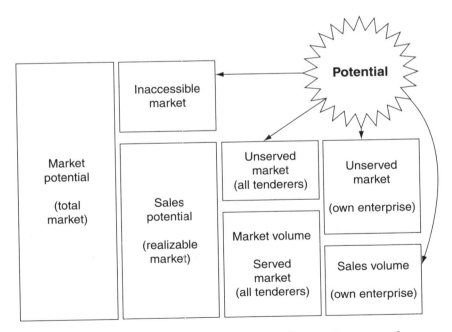

Figure 3.9   Market potential analysis using the market cascade
(following Kohloeffel (2000), p.131)

market is inaccessible. Access may not be possible because of, for instance, governmentally protected monopolies granted to competitors or because product certifications have not been granted. The remaining accessible market is then to be divided into the served and the unserved market. Non-served market segments exist for individual businesses because of a lack of market opening, non-available products and services or because of a non-competitive price / service ratio.

Workshop

The strategy focuses on all stages in the market cascade. In a workshop, questions regarding development of the potential target market deliver concrete strategic points of attack for business development (see Figure 3.10).

Workshop **Market potential analysis**			
Market cascade	How large is the market?	How can the market be described qualitatively?	How do we open up the market?
Market potential • What development is identifiable?			
Inaccessible market • Can the reason for the market being inaccessible be eliminated?			
Unserved market (all tenderers) • Which product/market segments are interesting?			
Unserved market (own business) • Is a penetration strategy possible?			
Sales volume • Is expansion possible (price/quantity policy)?			

Figure 3.10   Workshop: Market potential analysis

Tip

Data assessment is necessary for the analysis of market potential. In many sectors, one can make use of regularly released market research reports from industry groups, marketing research institutes or information brokers. Furthermore, a market model can be produced based on assumptions drawn from certain determining variables. For instance, the volume of a market segment and its further development depend on economic indicators, such as the development of pro capita income.

KEY QUESTION

How should the business position itself?

You must apply a strategy to achieve the upper hand in the world. Speed is of the essence. Make use of it when the other cannot reach you. Take the path he does not expect. Attack where he has let his guard down.

(Sun Tzu)

In practice, many approaches have been developed with which to attain success by working with the opportunities and risks provided by environments and competitive forces. Although each successful strategy is a unique entity, three basic strategies can be identified for product-related businesses. These are the strategies of cost leadership, differentiation and specialization. In addition, the strategies of the 'total customer solution' and the 'system lock-in' have to be taken into consideration as opportunities to create a cutting-edge position in the market.

Method

The strategy of cost leadership is targeted at realizing a significant cost advantage in a sector and is applicable to those markets in which price is the relevant criterion. The business can either lower the price and thus increase unit production or, at a stable price, increase its yield through cost reductions. This positioning strategy supports a series of approaches:

- To achieve success as the cost leader, a relatively high market share as the benchmark for a high cumulative production volume is necessary. According to the concept, the experience curve of the competitor with the largest cumulative production yield can achieve the lowest cost level and is the leader in terms of cost per unit. The smaller the competitor, the greater the potential difference in costs will be. Growth and volume thus become the most powerful lever for a successful strategy.

- The potential for lowering costs is realized through strict control of the cost targets, by avoiding marginal customers and by minimizing the relative costs in the individual value creation areas.

■ Cost leadership is often connected with mass production and standardized production.

■ Cost leadership requires setting up production plants with an efficient size.

The strategy of differentiation is aimed at clearly differentiating your own offering from the products and services of competitors by creating a clearly recognizable benefit for the customer and thus setting up a monopolistic playing field that permits higher prices. The focus is not directly on the costs but rather on the essential exclusivity of the offering. A strategy of exclusivity is frequently incompatible with a high market share in the sector because not all consumers are willing to pay a higher price for the additional features offered. The strategy of differentiation is thus directed at the entire sector, but in many cases it can only reach a limited segment of consumers. As an approach to differentiation, the following may be considered:

■ unusual product functions;

■ design;

■ high quality;

■ short delivery times;

■ unique technology;

■ excellent service;

■ well-established dealer network.

The strategy of specialization is used to apply a tightly focused group of concentrations. While the other two previously mentioned types of strategy are directed toward a cross-sector application of their goals, in this strategy the business concentrates on specific market segments with relatively homogeneous customer demand. The business is better able to fulfil this demand consistently than the competition. Because the economic advantage is achieved primarily through either a cost benefit or a usefulness benefit, this strategy may be interpreted as either a focused strategy to achieve cost leadership or as one of differentiation. The following niches come into question for this strategy:

- a specific consumer group;

- a specific portion of the production programme;

- a geographically isolated market.

The 'total customer solution' strategy (Hax/Dean) is based on a solution concept geared to improving the client's specific economic situation. The objective of this strategy is to develop intensive customer retention. A coherent offering of products and services is used to increase clients' ability to enhance their own economic advantage. Specifically, this means that the solution offered helps the client to increase sales revenues, lower operating costs or keep investment and hence the capital charge for business assets to a minimum. Unlike previous strategies, the important factor here is to develop and re-engineer an integrated value chain – all the way from the client to the supplier. The innovation process centres on development of the client's end-to-end business model.

The 'system lock-in' strategy includes in the creation of economic advantage not only the suppliers but also the so-called 'complementors', who supplement your offering with the addition of their products and services, thereby creating an even greater competitive edge among customers. The key to this strategy is to integrate the 'complementors' into a system-wide value chain and at the same time squeeze out competitors. This can be achieved, for example, by setting standards and creating exclusive sales and marketing channels. A high degree of acceptance and a large number of users are the pivotal factors for the success of this strategy.

The table opposite shows examples for the strategic success factors of these positioning strategies.

The points of attack for competitive strategies can be shown graphically in a 'strategy clock for positioning' (see Figure 3.11). The strategies are positioned relative to the variables of prices and observed value creation. Fields 1–5 show the starting point for successful positioning in order to adopt a strategic approach, fields 6–8 are profitable courses of action in a monopoly situation only.

Type of strategy	Strategic success factors	
	Required abilities/Means	**Organizational requirements**
Comprehensive lead in cost	Simple products Standardization Modularization High investments and access to capital Process innovations Cost optimization of the entire chain of value creation Use of platforms to lower costs	Intensive cost controlling Fine-tuned reporting system Clearly structured organization Quantitative orientated system of motivation Purposeful leadership
Differentiation	Customer awareness and customer relations management Outstanding marketing Product engineering Creativity and solutions competence Knowledge of the customer and the customer processes Basic research Technological mastery Use of cost-sinking platforms	Close coordination in the areas of research and development together with marketing System of awards recognizes the achieved value creation for the customer Acquiring and supporting the development of highly qualified, creative employees Competence programme for solutions competence and entrepreneurship Project management
Specialization	Combination of the abovementioned measures, directed at the specific strategic target	Combination of the above mentioned measures, directed at the specific strategic target
Total customer solution	Consulting skills Understanding of client's business model and processes Customer responsiveness and a high degree of trust on the part of the client	Direct customer contact Joint development with the client Integrated value chain (client, ourselves, suppliers)
System lock-in	System offering with the development of line-of-business and/or technology standards High degree of market penetration (client's installed base) Optimization of the performance of the system offered	Expansion of the integrated value chain with the incorporation of 'complementors' and the exclusion of competitors Exclusive sales and marketing channels

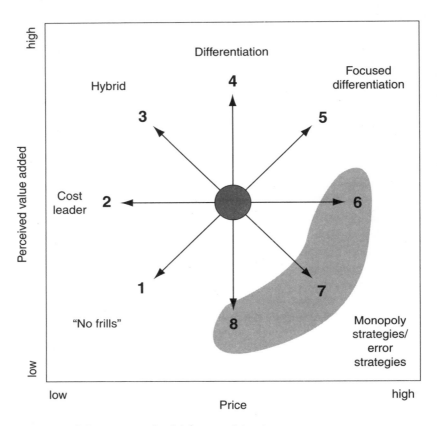

Figure 3.11   A 'strategy clock' for positioning

(according to Johnson/Scholes (2002), p.320)

Porter recommended that businesses should clearly opt for one of the strategies. This unequivocal positioning and the suitable business model is necessary to create competitive edge and a satisfactory business value. In view of the increasingly harsh market conditions of recent years, this position is increasingly subject to criticism. In the case of differentiation strategies, lowering costs through a multiple use of platforms as seen in the automobile industry has been encouraged. In today's fast-paced high technology branches, it is possible for many businesses to achieve an advantage over their competitors by simply switching between both strategic patterns of action. In this state of hyper-competition, the competitive advantage is increasingly found in the ability to successfully direct a series of interactions in the environment of the business and thus stay one step ahead of the competition. An example of a successful development using the strategy clock is the positioning strategy of Japanese car manufacturers in Europe. Between 1960 and 1970, the European market was first opened up (lower left position in the strategy clock on Figure 3.11 (position 1). The cars were cheap and were sold with limited value creation expectations. Between 1970 and 1980, the quality of the cars improved, the prices, however, were held at a relatively low level (positions 2 and 3). By the mid-1990s, a differentiation strategy was apparent (positions 4 and 5), demonstrated by the blanket provision of additional options (airbags, air conditioning, long-term warranties).

Workshop

In order to achieve a clear competitive edge, the ERRC method of Kim and Mauborgne can be used in the workshop. Within the four factors 'Eliminate, Reduce, Raise, Create', the focus is on identification of differentiating advantages (see Figure 3.12). These factors also help in finding starting points for the effective allocation of your own resources.

Workshop ERRC positioning	
Eliminate Which of the factors that the industry takes for granted should be eliminated?	**Raise** Which factors should be raised well above the industry's standard?
Reduce Which factors should be reduced well below the industry's standard?	**Create** Which factors should be created that the industry has never offered?

Figure 3.12   Workshop: ERRC positioning

(according to Kim/Mauborgne (2005), p.29)

Tip

When preparing your specific positioning strategies, take into account possible new directions of attack that your competitors might also adopt in the future. This will give you both the needed potential degree of freedom and also allow you to evaluate potential conflict situations in advance, relative to your chances of success.

KEY QUESTION

How can a balanced portfolio be developed?

He who can make use of strategically advantageous possibilities shall be victorious.

(Sun Tzu)

The term portfolio is derived from the French term *portefeuille*, which has two distinct meanings. On the one hand, a *portefeuille* is a container for keeping valuable documents, while on the other hand the term characterizes the administrative competences of a secretary, such as a Secretary of State.

For diversified businesses, the strategic business field may be seen as a portfolio within the framework of strategic planning. Strategic business fields can be delineated most clearly by the following characteristics or requirements:

■ They have an independent market task to perform, ie they are responsible for products or services for specific customers or market segments.

■ They compete in the marketplace with external competitors.

■ They are managed as business units, ie they have relative autonomy in terms of sales, development, production, personnel and investment responsibilities. From the perspective of overall controlling, in diversified businesses it is important to make sure that the appropriate synergy potentials between the strategic business units are identified and utilized.

Portfolio concepts belong to the core tools of strategic business planning and are used to address two levels of business development.

On the corporate level of the business, the planning for all the various business fields is undertaken. The strategic programme design lies in the connection between the business fields in which the business intends to be active and how these fields are to be prioritized. In this context, the entire activity field of the business is seen as a portfolio in which existing business fields are further developed and new fields added or dropped from a specific field.

At the level of the strategic business field, differentiated planning for each of the specific business fields is carried out. These business fields may be seen – to the extent that they encompass the above characteristics – as a business in miniature. This can be controlled using the timeframe derived variable of EVA®, cash flow, value creation, present value, etc. In order to maintain an edge over one's competitors, specific basic principles and guidelines for the development of competitive advantages on the customer or market side or in the functional areas of value creation need to be defined at this level.

In practice, a series of portfolio concepts, which have been developed by consultancies in collaboration with businesses, is applicable. All of these portfolio concepts take the strategic triangle as the basis for their approach (Figure 3.13). This is the dynamic relationship formed by the customer, the competitor and your own business. The customer will evaluate not only those products and services offered by your business on value for money, but also the offerings of competitors. Not only is an optimal configuration of this relationship strategically relevant, but also the achievement of a relative position of advantage with regard to competitors from the viewpoint of the customer. This relative position is the customer advantage, the pivotal element for strategic success. Taking the perspective of the customers into consideration, this advantage is of strategic importance when:

■ It concerns components of the product or the services that are important to the customer.

■ The advantage is perceptible to the customer.

■ The advantage is sustainable and can be safeguarded in the long term.

The core approach of portfolio characterizations is to portray the environmentally driven aspects (opportunity / risk) and the business driven aspects (strengths / weakness) in such a manner that respective dimensions may be visualized. The three portfolio concepts referred to in the following paragraphs are representative of the large number employed in actual practice.

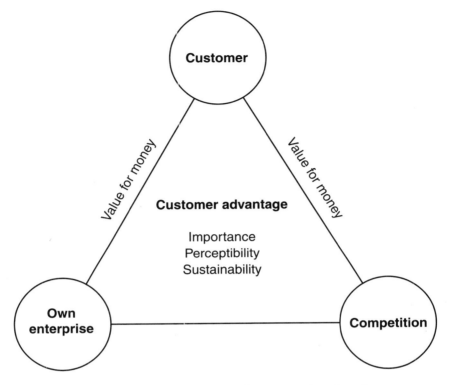

Figure 3.13 Customer advantages in the strategic triangle
(according to Ohmae (1982), p.72)

Method

Market share/market growth portfolio

The starting point for the market share/market growth portfolio developed by the Boston Consulting Group is the experience curve (the horizontal axis of the portfolio). The empirically calculated connection shows that the real unit cost of a product sinks each time by a constant amount (potentially 20–30 per cent) as soon as the cumulative output of the product doubles. The reasons for this are the learning effect, specialization effects and process innovations, etc. For the planning of strategic business fields, far reaching consequences arise from this connection. Securing a high relative market share becomes a core factor, as it is the only way to guarantee the long-term cost advantage as the basis for sustainable success. When, additionally, the concept of the product lifecycle is taken into consideration (the vertical axis of the portfolio), it becomes clear that securing high relative market share is best aimed for in markets with a high rate of growth. This is because the cumulative amounts grow rapidly in such markets and the corresponding dynamic cost digression effects are attainable. On this basis, a matrix with four fields can be derived (see Figure 3.14):

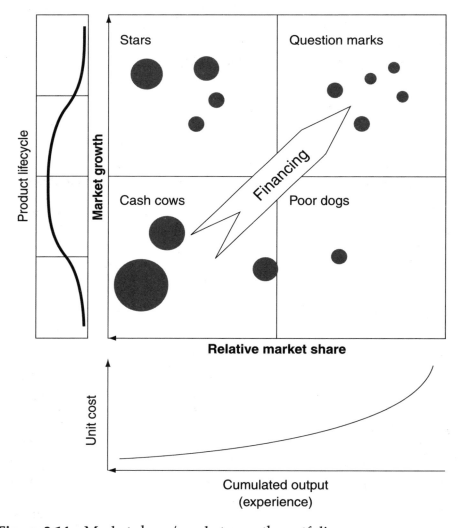

Figure 3.14 Market share / market growth portfolio
(according to Baum/Coenenberg/Guenther (1999), p.183)

- The question marks promise a high growth rate, but initially have a low market share and require financial resources in order to be developed to a critical point relative to market share.

- The stars show a high growth rate and are in a leading market position. They usually generate and require large financial resources and yield an above-average return.

- The cash cows show reasonable growth and deliver a large profit surplus.

- The poor dogs operate in stagnating or shrinking markets, have a mediocre to weak market position and generate no profit.

The standard strategies can now be derived for strategic management. In general, a differentiation can be made between the growth strategies (question marks), consolidating strategies (stars), milking strategies (cash cows) and disinvestment strategies (poor dogs). Regarding long-term development, the cash cows can deliver the financial means necessary for the development of the next generation of products and, under certain circumstances, the star products can do this as well. The target setting of sustainability requires that a well-balanced portfolio of options for present and future cash generators be available.

Product lifecycle – competitor's position portfolio

The starting point of this portfolio is the lifecycle concept developed by the Arthur D Little consultancy. This concept portrays the development of products, technologies and branches as time lines. This approach is based on the idea that in order to evaluate the attractiveness of a market, it is not enough to judge its growth rate alone, rather that its position within the lifecycle plays a decisive role relative to the potential for success. The corresponding lifecycle is therefore used as an external valuation factor. For the business based dimension, the competitive position is determined and classified in a range from weak to dominant. Apart from the standard strategies listed in Figure 3.15, this model can also be used to choose managers best fitted for the challenges of the product lifecycle relative to their personality profiles. Whereas creativity, improvisation and the ability to set up sustainable networks are desired qualities in the development phase, in later phases organizational talent and restructuring skills are needed. Viewed from the perspective of the lifecycle

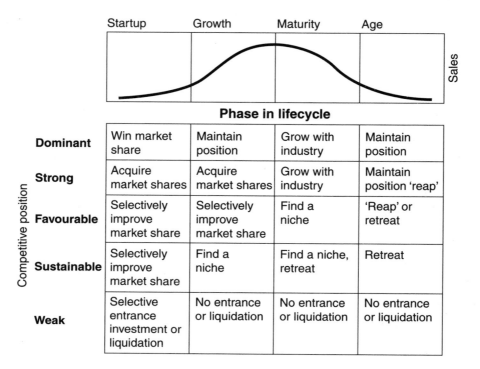

Figure 3.15   Product lifecycle – competitive position portfolio

(according to Hahn (1999), p.414)

phases of products and technologies, the need arises to balance the portfolio so that at any given time an adequate number of new options is available to guarantee continual business development. At the same time, continual development of the business is thus guaranteed and current cash generating products are used as a source for internal financing.

Technology portfolio

The existing portfolios represent those aspects of the market or the attractiveness of the sector in question. In contrast, aspects of the attractiveness of technology are specifically considered. In order to integrate these significant factors, the technology portfolio was developed–Figure 3.16. The concept makes it possible to take into consideration technology-driven aspects relative to the products as well as the process technology. The environmentally related technology attractiveness and the business relevant strength of the resources are to be taken into consideration.

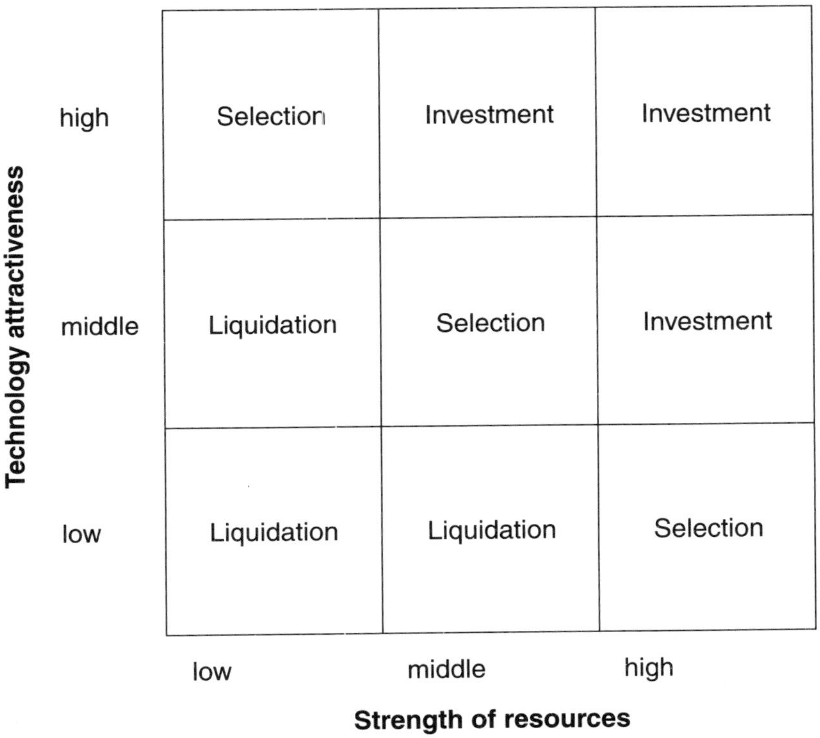

Figure 3.16 Technology portfolio

(according to Hahn (1999), p.417)

In order to measure the qualitative aspects of the attractiveness of the technology, the following aspects need to be examined:

- Compatibility. Should further possible technical developments with possible positive or negative consequences on other technologies used by the business be considered?

- Range of application. How is the expansion of further technical developments regarding the number of areas of application and the quantity in each of these areas to be judged?

- Further development potential. To what extent is technical advance and a resulting cost reduction or service quality increase possible?

The resource strengths are brought into play with regard to the following aspects:

- Technical qualitative degree of mastery. How are the applications based on the technology to be judged, both in their technical-commercial and their qualitative aspects? How deeply is the knowledge of the technology and its applications anchored in the business?

- Potentials. Are the financial, personal, objective and legal resources necessary for realizing the open potentials available?

- Reaction speed. How quickly can the business develop the existing capabilities for further development compared to its competitors?

The results may then be derived as standard strategies for investing and selecting as well as liquidating and disinvestment. They can be extended by considering the aspects of deciding and optimizing the application of research and development resources, by weighing the question of in-house production versus outsourcing, and by weighing the choice of a production site.

Workshop

In a workshop, using Figure 3.17, prepare a product lifecycle and competitive position portfolio for a product of your business. As described above, it is necessary for both the position in the product lifecycle and the competitive position to be evaluated. For the evaluation of the competitive position, you may make use of work already done in the workshops on industry attractiveness and competitor analysis.

Workshop Product lifecycle and competitive position			
Product/offer	Where does the product stand within the lifecycle?	How strong is the competitive position?	What is our approach?
Product 1			
Product 2			
Product 3			

Figure 3.17 Workshop: Product lifecycle and competitive position

Tip

Portfolio concepts are, without a doubt, an important aid in strategic management. Their essential advantages are found in the clear visualization of strengths, weaknesses, opportunities and risks as well as in the derivation of standard strategies to guarantee the survival of businesses. At the same time, these standard strategies must not be applied to the real world either lightly or as a matter of routine. They must, instead, be applied to each case in a relevant manner. Their applicability and the premises behind this application must be reconciled in order to fulfil the aims of the strategy.

4

Offer and Marketing

Focusing customer advantage

KEY QUESTION

Which product/market strategy is pursued?

Appear where your opponent cannot reach you. Fly to the place where he least expects you.

(Sun Tzu)

In this part of the book the customer oriented market strategy is placed centre stage. Creating customer advantage is the pivotal issue here. As a starting point a strategic approach must be developed for the product/market. In principle, there are two basic strategies: growth and survival. Survival strategies are indicated in times of a downturn in business development and when structural problems affect the sector. Growth strategies are directed toward increasing the potential share of an expanding market or increasing your own market share at the cost of your competitors.

Method

Ansoff (1984) has focused on growth strategies. Beginning with existing or possible new products and markets, he differentiates between four product/market strategies.

Market penetration

The point of attack consists of achieving a stronger penetration using current products in existing markets. This can be achieved through an increase in unit sales per consumer or through an expansion of the number of consumers by adopting aggressive price and communication policies. In a stagnating market, this strategy leads to an expansion of market share at the competitors' expense.

Market development

A second strategic option is to advance into new markets with existing products and services. Market penetration and market development strategies can entail offering new applications for existing products or opening up new market segments. In market development, the role market segmentation plays is of great importance. It permits a specific separation of markets and becomes, in this way, the basis for focusing the contributions of homogeneous stakeholders. These are formed in accordance with specific criteria. The table below lists possible segmentation criteria for consumer and industrial markets.

Aspect of segmentation	Consumer market	Industrial market
Customer characteristics	age, gender, origin, income, marital status, location, lifestyle	sectors, locations, size, technology, profitability, management
Purchasing behaviour	size of purchases, brand loyalty, necessity of purchase, selection criteria	volume, necessity of purchase, frequency of purchases, purchasing process, selection criteria, distribution channels
Preferences	price / quantity / quality preferences, time preferences, brand preferences	price / quantity / quality preferences, time preferences, service agreements, cooperative agreements in value creation process

Product development

This strategy focuses on developing products or solutions for existing markets. It must be taken into consideration that the degrees of innovation can vary considerably and are frequently influenced by customers' perceptions.

Diversification

Diversification introduces new products and services to new markets. There are three relevant diversification strategies:

■ Horizontal diversification. The new products are similar to the previous products. The actual connection can be based on existing

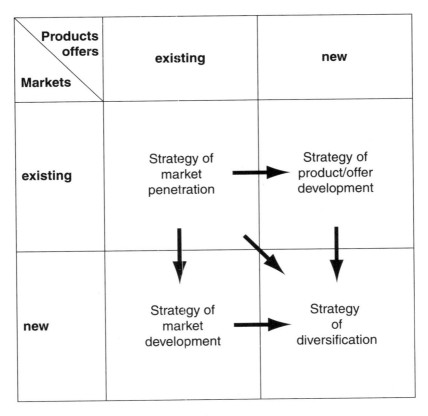

Figure 4.1   Product / market matrix

(according to Johnson/Scholes (2002), p.363)

production technology, the input factors used or the distribution channels. A typical advantage of this strategy lies in exploiting synergies through the takeover of a competitor with a similar value creation structure and complementary products.

■ Vertical diversification. This strategy expands your own action radius in earlier steps in the value creation chain (backward integration) or later steps in the value creation chain (forward integration). This results in an active change in the structure of the sector as well as in the competitive environment. This strategy aims at increasing independence from the bargaining strength of both suppliers and customers.

■ Lateral diversification. In such a strategy, there is no longer a direct connection to the previous product or market aspects. Free financial resources are invested in new segments under the aspect of risk diversification.

Workshop

In the workshop, use Figure 4.2 to analyse which strategies are possible and advantageous in the future opening of the product/market matrix. Begin with the strategy of market penetration. How can you succeed in increasing your own sales? What other possibilities are there to develop your product? Which new market segments have arisen and how can they be opened up? When working on these factors, remember that all strategies are only capable of realization with the appropriate expenditure of resources for product development or opening up of the market. To achieve sustainable success, there must also be competitive advantages. Which approach is the most promising: short term, mid term or long term?

Workshop Product/market strategy		
	Existing products/offers	**New products/offers**
Existing markets	Market penetration	Product/offer development
New markets	Market development	Diversification

Figure 4.2   Workshop: Product/market strategy

Tip

Look for sources of information to identify additional potentials in the organization first. At the beginning of the workshop, you are advised to talk to the experts in marketing, research and development, and sales. The central interfaces to the markets and thus to the customers are the sales employees or representatives. Their knowledge of market developments and customers' wishes needs to be collated, structured and processed. An especially promising approach to the development of product or market strategy is a comprehensive dialogue with selected customers regarding their current and future preferences.

KEY QUESTION

How are target segments opened up?

It is the unexpected which leads to victory.

(Sun Tzu)

A sustainable strategy for success lies in surprising the customer again and again with unique offers. Many businesses face the challenge of moving from product orientation to becoming market and customer oriented. This successful change can be supported by applying the basic rule of all marketing: the customers' needs are primary.

Method

The development of the product/market strategy was introduced in the previous section. Now, the strategy to open up the market is to be determined. This strategy is oriented to the success potential of the product/market segment. As Figure 4.3 indicates, the following is always possible:

■   To concentrate very specifically on certain product/market segments.

■   To choose the product/market segments selectively.

■   To specialize in certain markets or certain products.

■   To address the market as a whole.

A specific strategy for opening up a market segment is to be chosen for each of the selected market segments. A segment-specific marketing mix needs to be drawn up that consistently determines product, price, sales and communication policies.

Product policy

The goal is to distinguish oneself from the competition through a unique offer. Uniqueness provides a promising monopolistic playing field through a unique selling proposition (USP) for the business offering it. The prerequisite for this success is, however, that the uniqueness is relevant to the customer, is directly apparent and the customer is thus willing to pay

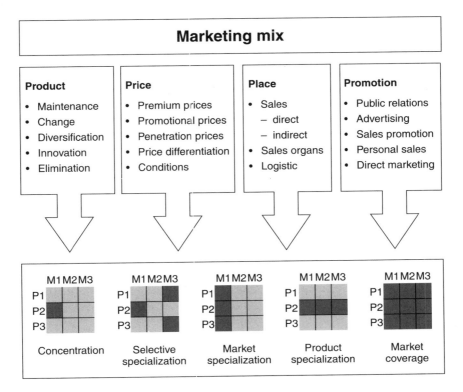

Figure 4.3   Opening up target segments

(following Kotler (2003), p.16)

for the additional value offered. The product policy formally begins with the design of the characteristics of the core product. These are such elements as equipment, quality, variations and design. In an expanded view of the product, it is possible to include further differentiation potential beginning with brand policy, packaging design and guarantee, and ending with service. From a strategic point of view, the decision needs to be taken within the framework of product policy as to whether the design of the product is to be retained or marginally changed and whether there are possibilities for diversification or innovation. The question must also be answered as to whether the product should perhaps be phased out.

Pricing policy

Pricing policy is dictated by what customers will pay. This is largely determined by the uniqueness of the offering. In addition to this, the following conditions are important for the price policy: credit conditions, rebates, supply and payment conditions, and financial models.

Suitable price strategies need to be derived for the opening up of the product/market segments. Basically, the following strategic options are applicable here.

Skimming strategy

This strategy aims at entering the market with high prices and then adding further layers of customers by gradually lowering the price. The prerequisite for this is a high differentiation level that addresses the wishes of the 'early adapters' (trendsetters, innovators).

Penetration strategy

This strategy, by contrast, sets the price as low as possible in order to achieve a maximum of market share as a barrier to counter the threat of powerful competitors entering the market. The goal is to tie into the widest customer base possible and to set the standards in the market.

Conditions policy

This is an increasingly important topic, especially in mature markets for product and services business. The high degree of similarity in prices often leads to price wars that drive businesses to the limit of their ability to survive. The determination of the conditions is an important criterion in differentiation. To present convincing arguments for the value of the product to the customer, it is helpful when one has an understanding of the customers' operative and strategic business drivers. The cost of capital has lately become an especially decisive argument. Both the price and the conditions policy can – reflecting the interests of the customer – be brought into the negotiations as bargaining factors. The following example from the brokerage of shares illustrates this principle. A deposit of 30 per cent of the value of the order to the sum of €10 million is, at an interest rate on capital of 10 per cent, a value creation of €300,000. This is equivalent to a rebate of 3 per cent on the volume of the order and can be used as a bargaining point in negotiations.

Distribution policy

Each vendor must decide how the product is to be placed in the target market. On the one hand, the business must determine the physical aspects pursuant to distribution, such as the locations, inventory management methods and means of transport. On the other hand, acquisition channels for the distribution and the means of transport have to be defined. Today, only a few businesses sell their products directly. Most make use of at least one, if not a multi-layered, channel of distribution. The following questions have to be answered in the decision-making process about distribution policy:

- Customer – How many customers are there? Where are they located? In accordance with which buying habits do they make their purchases? How open are they to new sales methods?

- Product – How non-intuitive is the product? How often is it used? How sensitive to transportation risks is it? How well will it be warehoused?

- Channels of distribution – What are the dimensions of the sales-related and physical aspects of the distribution channel? Is it possible to negotiate these aspects? Is it relevant to establishing a relationship with the customer?

- Competition – How are competitors' products designed? Through which channels are they distributed?

- Business – How good is the financial position of your own business? What experience, strengths and weaknesses does it have in the distribution process?

- Environment – Which legal regulations are to be taken into account?

- Communication policy – What messages are conveyed to the target segment? As possible instruments, the areas of public relations, advertising, merchandising, individual sales and direct marketing come into consideration. The point of attack of the communication policy can be summed up for all of these instruments with the AIDA (attention, interest, desire, action) approach. This means: Awaken the potential customer's attention. Create a sense of interest. Increase the desire to own the product. Finally, motivate the customer to take action and buy.

Workshop

In the workshop, first choose the appropriate segment criteria for your business strategy. Then identify possible market segments using Figure 4.4. Which segments appear promising to you? In evaluating this question, the aspects discussed above regarding the sector attractiveness and the strengths and weaknesses of your business must to be considered. Define an appropriate marketing mix for each of the segments.

Workshop Market opening strategies				
Segmentation criteria:				
Segment	**Marketing mix**			
	Product Product policy	Price Price and conditions policy	Place Distribution policy	Promote Communication policy
Segment 1				
Segment 2				
Segment 3				
Segment ...				

Figure 4.4   Workshop: Market opening strategies

Tip

The strategic decision about the marketing mix is not an isolated, limited decision. The tools used need to support the chosen positioning effectively. At the same time, their effect on other aspects of the marketing mix must be taken into account. In practice, the following critical questions have proven helpful in optimizing the marketing mix:

■ Are the tools consistently aimed at the positioning?

■ What cost/performance ratio is to be expected from the individual measures?

■ How will the competition behave?

5

Knowledge and Competences

Establishing strategic strength

KEY QUESTION

Which core competences guarantee success?

Invincibleness lies within you, vulnerability in the opponent.
(Sun Tzu)

The main focus of this strategy is directed at the question of how sustainable competitive advantages may be achieved. In previous considerations, the driving forces of the environment and the market based view were pre-eminent. In order to exploit all potentials for success, it is necessary to focus on the internal side of things. The resource based view is focused on available and developed resources as well as competences within the business.

The term 'resources' encompasses the material components of the objective and financial capital. The term 'competences' refers to such non-tangible aspects of human capital as know-how and other aspects with which the business is able to achieve organizational or technical objectives. Sustainable competitive advantages can only be achieved and defended if, in competition about cost, quality and time, these hidden, business-specific resources and competences make an advantageous position possible. The targeted development of these resources and abilities exploits not only current sources of competitive edge but permits the business to react flexibly to changes over time. Finally, it is these resources and competences that make a competitive, offensive structure possible.

Top management has the task of improving core competences through identification, development, integration, use and transfer of these resources and competences. Core competences and the strategic advantage they provide are described below.

Strategic significances of core competences are:

■ Core competences are customer relevant.

■ They lead to a perceptible and proven competitive edge.

■ This is demonstrated by the customers' willingness to pay.

■ They may be difficult for the competition to imitate or attack, eg those associated with tacit knowledge.

Strength of the business relative to core competences are:

■ Core competences are transferable to other product and market combinations and internal functions and so provide strategic leverage for the entire business.

■ They are permanently available to the business.

■ They are well organized within the business processes.

The development and maintenance of core competences must, in the final analysis, lead to a value creating sale of products and services in the consumer markets. A case in point: at Canon, the three core competences of precision mechanics, optics and microelectronics form the basis for the development of the entire product range, from colour photocopiers to digital cameras.

The approach of core competences can be portrayed as a 'system tree' (Figure 5.1). Core competences have a double function: they nourish the

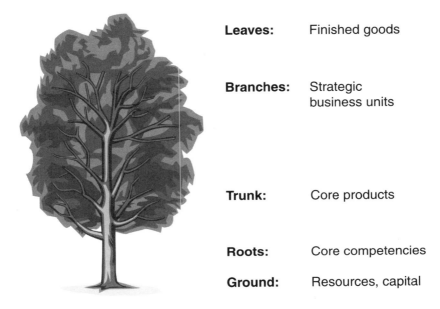

Leaves:	Finished goods
Branches:	Strategic business units
Trunk:	Core products
Roots:	Core competencies
Ground:	Resources, capital

Figure 5.1   Core competencies in the analogy of a 'system tree'
(following Hamel/Prahalad (1990), p.314)

tree dynamically with the resources and give the trunk, or core products, a stable backbone over the long term. The trunk divides into branches, strategic business units, which have entrepreneurial responsibility. On these branches the leaves, the finished goods, grow. While the leaves have relatively short, annual, lifecycles, the roots and trunk sustain long-term growth. To complete the analogy, they, too, need the continuous care of the gardener – investment by the entrepreneur.

Method

The question for management is to identify the core competences that are relevant to competition, evaluate them, develop them and use them. On the one hand, customers deliver ideas because they are interested in their own advantage, as seen through use oriented feedback. On the other hand, the business attempts to develop new solutions and applications through its own offerings.

The core competence portfolio is structured along these two dimensions: first, the strategic significance of the core competence and, second, the strength of the business relative to this core competence. It may be used as an instrument for deriving the resource based strategic decisions:

■ In sector I (low strength, low strategic significance) there is a gap in competences that is of little significance. The standard strategy here is to stop investing in this sector and buy in competences from partners.

■ In sector II (low strength, high strategic significance) there is a pressing need for action to fill a gap in competences. This can be accomplished through a know-how transfer from other sectors of the business and through acquisitions and strategic alliances. Within such a collaborative framework, the necessary investment is a given.

■ In sector III (high strength, little strategic significance) there is no opportunity to achieve a direct competitive edge through further

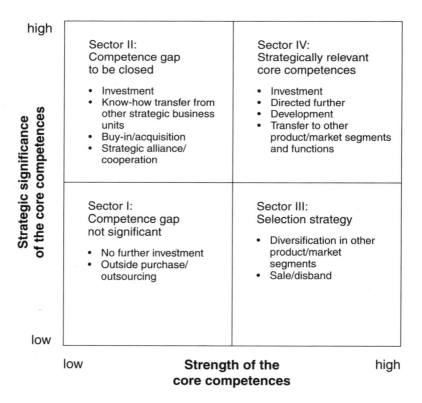

Figure 5.2   Strategic core competences portfolio

(according to Hahn (1999), p.953)

business activity. This high degree of strength can be put to use through diversification to set up an alternative product/market segment. In addition, there is the opportunity to sell the area of competence if there is little strategic significance.

- Sector IV (high strength, great strategic significance) provides the fundamental basis for present and future competitive advantages. The standard strategy here is to focus on the further development of competences. Additionally, the product/market segments and the functional areas should be analysed to determine whether this core competence can be used on a wider basis in the business.

Workshop

In the workshop, the core competences of the business must first be identified. In a second step, an evaluation of these core competences is performed using Figure 5.3. The analysis is based on the competences identified, their strategic significance and the strength of the business relative to these competences. Finally, the strategies for the development of core competences can be derived from the standard strategies.

Workshop Core competences analysis			
Which core competences create competitive edge?	What is the strategic significance of the core competence? • relevance • creating competitive edge • difficult to imitate	How strong is the core competence? • transferable • permanently available • well organized	How do we proceed?
Competence 1			
Competence 2			
Competence 3			

Figure 5.3   Workshop: Core competence analysis

Tip

Remember that the market based view and the resource based view are not opposites, but rather perspectives that complement each other perfectly. In a further step, try to derive competence profiles for functions or employees based on these core competences. In this way, you will be certain that personnel development and further education are not only present as incentives but are of direct value to the customer oriented requirements of the business.

KEY QUESTION

How is knowledge made available?

Those whose generals are competent will succeed.

(Sun Tzu)

Knowledge has a unique characteristic. Unlike all the other potential factors, the more it is used, the more it increases. This is especially true for the service and solution business where knowledge is the basis for success. From the strategic perspective, the goal is to leverage knowledge to create more competitive advantages. This task can only be achieved when knowledge management is anchored as a permanent element in the business. So knowledge management is the organizational instrument for the sustainable deployment of core competences.

Method

Probst, Raub and Romhardt (1999) categorize knowledge management into eight component fields:

- Knowledge identification – achieving transparency regarding strategically relevant internal and external fields of knowledge, based on data, information and abilities.

- Knowledge objectives. Concrete knowledge goals are to be developed for all levels in the business. Standard knowledge is drawn from the knowledge culture and the classification and development of existing abilities. Strategic knowledge goals define the need for organizational core knowledge in order to guarantee competitive ability and to set up appropriate business systems. The operative knowledge goals are reflected in a strategy oriented implementation of those building blocks of knowledge management in all functional sectors.

- Knowledge acquisition. Knowledge can be acquired through exchange with all internal and external partners, through the recruitment of experts, and through purchasing other businesses.

- Knowledge development – developing new ideas and abilities that form the basis for new products and more efficient processes. This does not only involve divisions that deal with the development of knowledge, eg research and development or market research, but also all employees and functional sectors. Especially critical for success is a culture oriented approach, one which makes creativity and innovation possible.

■ Knowledge distribution – the process of distributing available knowledge in the business. It is important to set up speedy and standard methods of distribution that make it possible to maintain a defined level of quality.

■ Knowledge use. Knowledge is only of value if it can be applied. The applications need to be defined and made available.

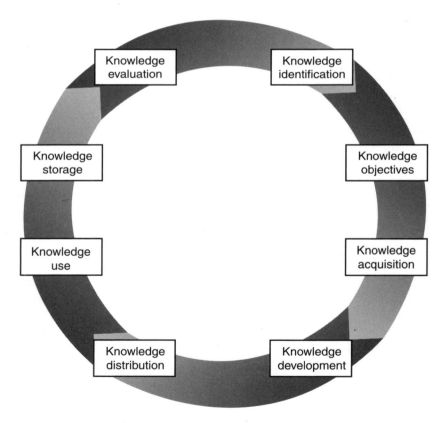

Figure 5.4   Building the circle of knowledge management
(according to Probst/Raub/Romhardt (1999), p.26)

■ Knowledge storage – the effective storage of documents, information and experience. The storage of knowledge can be supported and furthered through information-specific memory systems and through the appropriate culture of knowledge.

■ Knowledge evaluation. Knowledge must be continuously reviewed with respect to its effectiveness relative to the strategy. Because the strategy must be adjusted to fit the environment, the portfolio of central fields of knowledge must be constantly evaluated and, where necessary, updated. Knowledge evaluation thus closes the circle of knowledge management.

Workshop

The first step in this workshop, using Figure 5.5, is to identify the strategically relevant field of knowledge. Building on this, the next step is to work out how knowledge is acquired, developed and permanently stored. With the application of knowledge firmly in mind, the next step is to clarify how this knowledge can be used and distributed in the organization.

Workshop Knowledge management		
Which fields of knowledge are relevant to success?	How can the knowledge be acquired, developed and stored?	How is the knowledge used and distributed in the organization?
Field of knowledge 1		
Field of knowledge 2		
Field of knowledge 3		
Field of knowledge ...		

Figure 5.5   Workshop: Knowledge management

Tip

Together with external sources of knowledge there are a number of islands of knowledge in the business. These islands are only available to a few employees. Prior to buying into expensive external knowledge, the organization should be examined for existing sources of information. These islands of knowledge should be appropriately networked.

A further recommendation is to apply the results drawn from benchmarking analyses in order to create your own, unique knowledge position.

6

Value Chain and Organization

Delivering competitive advantages

KEY QUESTION

How is the value creation achieved?

The forces must be strategically placed. They must be in accordance with that which is advantageous.

(Sun Tzu)

The design of the process of value creation in a business at the level of functional activities has the potential of setting up sustainable competitive edge over competitors. Porter's value chain concept (1996) can be applied here as an instrument of strategy.

Method

In his approach to the value chain analysis, Porter (1996) distinguishes between primary and secondary activities. Primary activities are those directly aimed at the production and sale of a product or service. Secondary activities provide direction and support for primary activities.

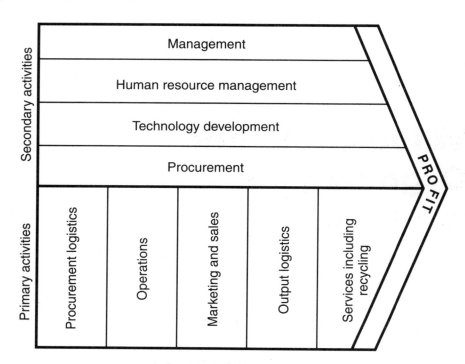

Figure 6.1   The value chain

(following Porter (1996), p.62)

Primary activities

■ 'Procurement logistics' comprises all activities that have an effect on the receipt, warehousing and provision of production facilities and materials.

■ 'Operations' means all activities within the framework of production. These include materials processing, intermediate warehousing, quality control, packaging, etc.

■ 'Marketing and sales' are the activities arising from the operative implementation of product policies, price policies, distribution policies and communication policies.

■ 'Output logistics' comprises physical distribution, delivery and setup of the products and services.

■ 'Service' includes activities that are intrinsic in maintaining value and consistently acquiring customers. In recent years, this model of value creation steps has been expanded to include waste management and recycling.

Secondary activities

■ 'Management' includes activities such as strategic planning, accounting, cash management, information and communication systems, and controlling systems.

■ The 'human resources management' sector is responsible for hiring, personnel development and the placement of employees.

■ Activities in 'technology development' are directed both at the product and at the process development. These include activities in the sector of research and development, process design and communication platforms.

■ 'Procurement' organizes the provision of necessary raw or pre-processed materials and the operating resources for all sections of the value chain.

The interfaces between the pre- and post-value chains from supplier to customers are of strategic importance alongside the concrete setup of the primary and secondary activities. This is of great importance because it is from these 'border crossings' that new structures and networking of the value creation arise. These are frequently advantageous to the strategic position. Using the value chain approach, differentiated benchmarking between competitors in an industry is possible. The application of the value chain concept makes it possible to identify the interaction between strengths and weaknesses in these activities. If a business is active in several strategic business fields, the value chain analysis can also be used to identify possible potentials for synergy effects – from the transfer of know-how to the joint use of value-creating activities.

The strategic aspects of the core competences are driving the value chain that can be applied to the decision of 'make' or 'buy'. Strategically, the decision to produce the good or service yourself has priority when trade secrets are involved and the core competences can be used to achieve

Advantages of 'make'	Advantages of 'buy'
• Concentration on strategic ongoing development of core competences • Keeping key and leading edge technologies secret • Utilization of available capacities • Direct control of processes • Establishment of total quality management • Less dependency on external factors	• Strategic concentration on core business and outsourcing • Use of the innovation potential of the supplier • Increasing flexibility and risk transfer • Scheduling security through just-in-time contracts • Improvement of liquidity because of reduced investment in business assets • Payroll advantages over in-house employees

competitive edge. The table shows the aspects relevant to the 'make' or 'buy' decision.

The value chain can be considered from the customer's point of view. The interaction of the individual components in the value chain ultimately leads to a value-for-money relationship perceptible to the customer. Through comparison with competitors, allocating the absolute and relative cost variables in the activity areas of the value chain can help to optimize the strategic configuration of the design of processes.

Workshop

In the workshop, using Figure 6.2, the following aspects of the value chain can be ascertained:

- the concrete design of the value creation stages;

- an analysis of the sectors in which core competence must be anchored;

- an analysis of the sources of competitive edge;

- the derivation of strategic points of attack relative to self-production, outsourcing and the choice of a production site for specific activity sectors.

Workshop Value chain and functional strategy			
Which phases does our value creation have?	Which phases do our core competences have?	What do we know about the best in class business? What competitive advantages do we achieve?	What are we purchasing?

Figure 6.2   Workshop: Value chain and functional strategy

Tip

Be creative in working with Porter's concept of the value chain. Define the strategic challenges and specialties of your business to form your own, personalized value chain. Productive ideas often occur when 'playing' with this approach.

KEY QUESTION

What is an effective organization?

Management of a large number of people is the same as management of a small number of people. They need to be separated into groups. Strength and weakness is a question of formation.

(Sun Tzu)

The core of the strategic organization is the fundamental determination of task structures for business executives and employees according to function, products and/or regions. Additionally, the authority and responsibilities of those in charge of the business units must be regulated.

The strategic goal setting of the business is focused on the potential for success. This is the creation of business value through a sustainable, successful offering of market oriented products and/or services. This superior goal can be concretized to the purpose of organizational design through specific subordinate goals. The adaptability of an organization to increasingly rapid changes in environmental conditions takes on a special meaning in this context. To guarantee the desired degree of flexibility, the requirements for the organizational model are:

■ market and competitive orientation;

■ innovative ability;

■ effectiveness of the management process;

■ efficiency of the business processes;

■ improvement of motivation;

■ resource efficiency.

Method

A concrete organization is a system of tasks, authorities, responsibilities, motivations, controls and the mutual exchange of information. These are the basis from which the successful implementation of the strategy is to be achieved. In the design of such a system there are six forms of organization that come into question. After defining these, this section will also look at strategic business units.

Linear organizations

In the linear organization, the entrepreneurial competence is concentrated on members of the management team, who know all of the relevant aspects of the market as well as the creation of value. Employees are given directions to follow. This strategy can easily be adapted to suit environmental conditions. In practice, this form is used in small businesses and in small strategic business units. The advantage of increased flexibility is countered by the uncertainty factor of the entrepreneur, since success is dependent to a high degree on his or her competence.

Functional organizations

A functional organization is necessary when as a result of increasing growth the complexity of tasks increases and the entrepreneur is no longer able to master all of them. Through the delegation of specific tasks, this model gives the entrepreneur the necessary elbow room for business polices and strategic tasks that are his or her responsibility as well as allowing him or her to coordinate functional areas more effectively. The optimal application point for a functional organization is within a clearly defined field of business activity. An organizational unit that markets a clearly defined range of products/services is focused on a specific market segment and competes against a specific group of competitors.

Divisional organizations

As a consequence of further diversification in new product/market segments, both the size and the complexity of the organization increase. The divisional organization consists of business units that are functionally structured around certain product lines and assume a coordinating and synergetic role in the central positions.

Matrix organizations

In the matrix organization, 'intrapreneurs' are charged with the management of a business unit, several functional areas or regional projects, or with a product line. Individuals from various functional areas, regional units and levels of responsibility can cooperate on complex tasks. The advantages in theory must be weighed against practice, since there are often coordination problems at the interfaces in the matrix.

Project and network organizations

Project and network organizations require the creation of an integrated structure in which the functional areas are more transparent and directed by the expectations of the consumers. The business becomes an unlimited network of individuals from various functional areas. Hierarchical levels and regional units work together to achieve value creation for the relevant stakeholders. This organizational form is predicated on all managers and employees thinking and dealing across all operative functions and hierarchies. The goal here is to achieve a new order of business processes with which the rules of the game in the market can be changed and customers are, comparatively speaking, better satisfied than by the organization's competitors.

Holding organizations

The holding organization places a number of legally distinct businesses under one management. The management of the holding can achieve value creation for the organization through various levers: through strategic portfolio management, the creation of synergies, increasing expandability and using financial advantages. An essential challenge for this form of organization lies in bringing decentralized entrepreneurial responsibility into line with an overriding universal strategy.

Strategic business units

The creation of strategic business units is of increasing importance to the business organization in dynamic markets. The units under consideration here are the ones that have been delegated the task of formulating and carrying out specific strategies by management. The task of business management is not the direct leadership of operations but the separation of the business into a series of strategic business units while coordinating them within an overall strategy. The determination of the absolute and relative variables of the strategic business units, their overlapping in markets and functions, their absolute number as well as their organizational integration, count as one of the most difficult tasks of business management. This is because these decisions, to a large extent, determine the sustainable success potential of the business.

A strategic business unit:

- produces and markets a precisely defined group of products or services;

- concentrates on a specific market or customer segment;

- competes with a strategic group of competitors;

- can achieve sustainable competitive edge through clear core competences;

- has control over the key functions of the value creation chain;

- is the central point for the integrated decisions that affect yield directly;

- pursues the goal of optimizing customer edge and thus provides a contribution to the increase in value of the business.

Two fundamental approaches can be followed in setting up strategic business units (see Figure 6.3). The segment based approach differentiates according to the market segments to be addressed and identifies the core competences to be established on that basis. These then result in appropriate consumer goods. The advantage of this approach lies in the considerable marginalization between the market segments to be processed. The resource based approach derives from its current future core competences the core products, which are then brought to market through strategic business units in the form of products and solutions. The benefit of this approach is that competitive advantages can be built on unique competences. The art of management lies in evaluating the possibilities and limitations of both approaches in a specific business and then deciding which approach is more likely to be successful. The competence portfolio that will be required in the future needs to be determined for both concepts. It must be developed in such a manner that leading positions in attractive markets can be achieved.

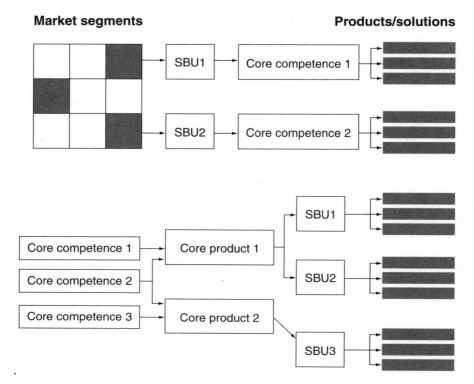

Figure 6.3   Setting up strategic business units (SBUs)

(following Hamel/Prahalad (1990), p.24)

Workshop

Different types of organizational models can be evaluated using the decision matrix (Figure 6.4) if the goal of organizational flexibility mentioned above is respected. The essential goals (eg laws or internal principles) must first be taken into consideration when considering alternative organizational options. If this is not the case, these essentials can be entered in the decision matrix and the goals compared with one another. In the evaluation phase, it is important to be certain that the effects of each goal are comparable to the others and an appropriate weighting factor is defined for these goals.

Workshop Organization	Which criteria are used to evaluate the organization?						
	Market and competitive orientation	Innovation capability	Effectiveness of the management process	Efficiency of the business processes	Motivation improvement	Resource efficiency	Evaluation
Linear organization							
Functional organization							
Divisional organization							
Matrix organization							
Project/ network organization							
Holding organization							

Figure 6.4   Workshop: Organization

Tip

From the subsidiary through the organizational model to top management, conflicts can be reduced if decision makers are involved early enough in the following processes: formulating goals, defining alternative organizational models, predicting impact and evaluating it.

KEY QUESTION

Which culture can support the strategy?

The Tao of the organization: to attain success in both the hard and the soft. This is how the clever strategy supports cooperation in a group.

(Sun Tzu)

The strategic process of transformation can be greatly advanced or, just as significantly, hindered by the business's culture. The culture of a business is a 'soft factor' that is difficult to grasp. This is especially true if the observers are themselves a part of the organization. The mission statements, orders or business reports of an organization formulate values, convictions and paradigms. They are only a clue to possible cultural aspects. These are often different from the business culture in practice. It must also be taken into consideration that within a business there is more than one culture. Certain subcultures can be found that have an influence on the change processes. This phenomenon can show itself when businesses have expanded through consolidations with other businesses and different cultures confront one another in the integration process. The culture of a business is a central success factor in the implementation of strategy.

Method

Ambrosini, Johnson and Scholes' net of business culture (1998) is a tool for investigating values, convictions and paradigms, their forms and their influence on strategy implementation. To this end, the following areas are taken into consideration.

Paradigms are the implicit concepts that are treated as if they were natural laws. They develop over a long period of time in and with the organization. They show themselves in the convictions that are closely tied to the value systems of the business. Because of their direct influence on behaviour and the development of structures, they stand in the centre of the cultural analysis. As, however, it is difficult to explicitly define these paradigms directly, the attempt must be made to determine their concrete character indirectly. This indirect approach deals with their appearance in stories, status symbols, power structures, organizational structures, control systems, rituals and routines.

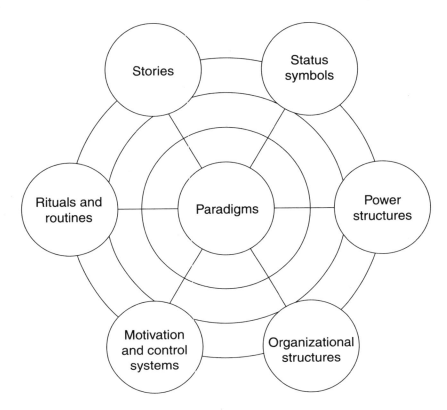

Figure 6.5 The net of business culture

(following Johnson/Scholes (2002), p.230)

Stories that are told about the organization and its employees are significant: an impression may be gained over what is seen to be important to or at variance with the value system. These stories typically broach the issues of success and failure, heroes and victims, and the limits of 'proper' behaviour.

Status symbols, such as the office fittings of managers at various levels of the hierarchy, company cars, job descriptions, logos, and how easily all of these may be achieved, are clear hints of the value and reward system of the business as well as its flexibility and ability to embrace change.

Existing power and organizational structures are the result of the fundamental assumptions of management and paradigms around the 'key to success' for management positions in the business.

The existing motivation and control systems provide success variables that are considered concrete values and have a significant influence on behaviour. These are, for instance, the coupling of management bonuses to the business value achieved through the implementation of a control system. This is seen as a central success factor for creating 'entrepreneurs' in the business.

Rituals and routines anchor values, basic beliefs and convictions in business-specific processes and systems. In this way, the dimensions of a business mission statement can, for instance, be reflected in the contents of training programmes, in the performance review systems or in the target agreement systems.

Workshop

In the workshop, six areas of business culture are examined, using Figure 6.6 to discover which of them support and which hinder strategy implementation. Based on this analysis of the situation, starting points for strategic development and promotion of the culture can be derived.

Workshop Culture			
Appearance	What supports the implementation?	What handicaps the implementation?	How do we develop our culture?
Stories			
Status symbols			
Power structures			
Organization structures			
Motivation and control systems			
Rituals and routines			

Figure 6.6   Workshop: Culture

Tip

To produce a comprehensive picture of the business culture, it is helpful to have the opinion of a mixed target group. Only when the interaction of the 'outside view' is taken together with the 'inside view' are the conditions met to permit the identification of 'blind spots' in your own perception, the recognition of all cultural driving factors, and the evaluation of their influence on strategy implementation.

7

Measures and Controlling

Managing implementation

KEY QUESTION

How is the implementation controlled?

Those whose upper and lower ranks follow the same goal will be victorious.

(Sun Tzu)

The central problem facing many businesses is effective and efficient implementation of strategy. The primary challenge of business management is to communicate corporate strategy throughout all levels of the business, to make it relevant to all the stakeholders. Putting strategy into practice, that is, formulating and communicating goals and milestones, is an important task that managers often find difficult. This task is important for individual departments, sections and employees to understand the direct impact of their efforts on strategy implementation. That this is often barely achieved, if not completely lacking, can frequently be traced back to the fact that the upper management level itself has no vision with regard to the business strategy. Such statements as 'We strengthen our customer orientation and thus become end-to-end solution providers' can be interpreted in various ways. If management doesn't have a clear goal and a fundamental consensus on how to achieve that goal, the results are friction and sluggish implementation. It has been the experience of many different consultants that management implicitly lacks a fundamental and common agreement. Given the high degree of competitive dynamics in today's market, this can threaten an organization's existence.

Method

Kaplan and Norton's Balanced Scorecard© (BSC) is an instrument that supports a well-balanced implementation of strategy (Kaplan and Norton, 1996). The underlying idea is that shareholder goals are coupled with customer expectations. The internal processes are coupled with learning. This results in a comprehensive perspective. The actions of an organization are seen as a balance of four viewpoints: financial, business processes, customers and markets, employee and innovation. These are plotted on a clearly laid out scorecard, which is often drawn in the form of a cockpit (Figure 7.1). This instrument combines qualitative and quantitative measurements, while taking into account the expectations of the various interest groups (eg customers, employees, suppliers, shareholders). The success of a strategy is measurable by checking results against the number of business goals that have been attained.

The traditional key data for financial breakdowns are based on past performance (eg EVA®, cash flow, sales) and are enhanced with future oriented key data (eg MVA). Results are not only coupled to short-term yields but also to the manner in which the processes, innovations and growth in the organization are set up, as well as the way customers evaluate the business unit. The result is a 'well-balanced' view of the organization with the goal of achieving sustainable yield. The table on page 100 contains specimen variables for scorecard dimensions.

The development of a BSC enables strategies to be expressed in concrete goals and metrics. This makes it possible for management to achieve consensus on which key strategic points are to be achieved. The further development process is useful throughout all business levels in order to understand and support the strategy and its consequences. It also supports the continuous evaluation of implementation. Feedback on strategy formulation is, of course, not excluded but, on the contrary, desired. BSCs can be prepared to give examples for all levels of an entire business or for a strategic business unit, for each division and even for individual areas of responsibility. BSCs can also be developed for completely new businesses and for joint ventures. Experience has shown that through this, strategies become more concrete and this prevents wasting time on worthless projects.

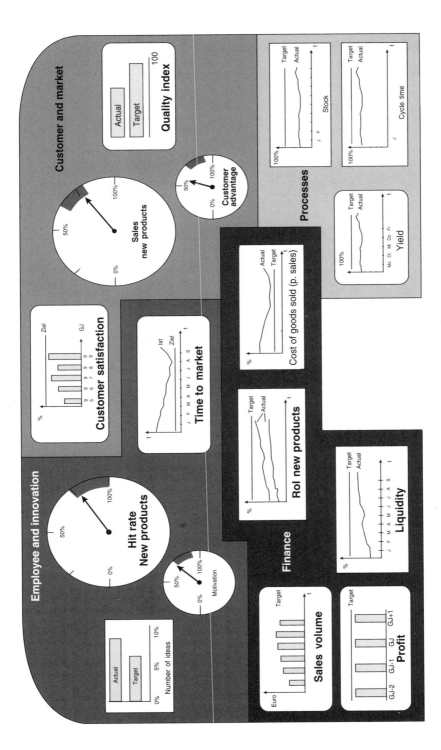

Figure 7.1 The balanced scorecard (BSC) as a management cockpit

(following Kohloeffel (2000), p.47)

Perspective	Strategic goal	Metric	Concrete value
Customer	Image as innovator	Sales of product introduced in the last year	> 55 %
	Customer loyalty	Sales share to repeat customers	> 75 % for the 10 largest customers
	New market acquisition segment X	Relative market share segment X	> 1 in 2 years
Internal business process	Time to market	Time lag on R&D projects	> 95% projects without delay
	Early tie-in of customers to R&D	Consulting hours in the 'design' phase	Increase to 10% of orders
	Speedy installation	Working days between winning bid and installation	95% under 20 days
Learning/ growth	Technology leadership	Number of patents in cutting-edge technology XYZ	> 3 for the coming year
	Use of common knowledge base	Number of networking employees	100% by the end of the business year
	Employee satisfaction	Index on basis of standardized questionnaires	Index > 75
Financial	Grow faster than the market does	Sales growth	Sales rate 50% over market growth
	Independence from capital market	Reducing accounts receivable	Commitment period of accounts receivable < 15 days
	Creation of business value	EVA®	EVA® > €5 million growth at 5% p.a.

Workshop

Before a BSC can be prepared, goals have to be clearly set and there must be a basic understanding of the concept. The process begins by establishing the business units for which a BSC is to be prepared. The orientation to vision and strategy requires a top–down procedure in setting up the BSC. The BSC is based on a strategy that must be previously defined. In order to process strategic goals specific to a business unit, interviews with top management ought to be conducted individually. The identified value generators (eg improvement in service, increasing customer identification management, growth through strategic acquisitions, technological leadership, cost-optimizing production) can also be taken as a basis to formulate the business's strategic goals. A large range of possible aspects to measure usually results. The challenge is to reduce these to a manageable number (between 15 and 25) and to identify the cause / effect interactions in the key data. Another series of interviews with all stakeholders is then recommended in order to produce a truly 'well-balanced' BSC draft.

Kaplan and Norton suggested the four dimensions mentioned above for the BSC: financial, business processes, customers and markets, employee and innovation.

Develop a BSC for your own business. The following workshop suggestions provide a framework for all fields described in this book. Which value generators are relevant to your own business? Be creative in transferring your own specific business and situation to the BSC.

Characteristic	Check
Concise	Is the aspect being measured focused on a value generator or a goal?
Measurable	Is the metric quantifiable?
Appraisable	Can the starting values and target values be derived?
Controllable	Can target value achievements for the metric be controlled by those responsible?
Reproducible	Can the metric be determined at regular intervals?
Non-overlapping	Have you avoided redundancy?

Tip

Take great care in defining the individual metrics. The method of calculating sources of data and reporting formats in addition to reporting
intervals needs to be clearly defined in a master data list. The metrics for
the individual variables often present problems. This is an aspect that
must be taken into account in the definition. The aspects of metrics
shown in Figure 7.2 should be fulfilled.

Workshop BSC/Controlling of strategy implementation					
Perspective/design field	Metric (Definition)	Current value	Target value	Measure	Responsible
Environment and positioning					
Offer and marketing					
Knowledge and competences					
Value chain and organization					
Measures and controlling					
Leadership and mobilization					
Finance and evaluation					
Opportunities and risk					

Figure 7.2   Workshop: BSC/Controlling of strategy implementation

KEY QUESTION

How is the degree of implementation measured?

The strategy ensures that instructions can be carried out consistently.
This makes the relationship between the leader and the led satisfactory.

(Sun Tzu)

One of the greatest challenges in increasing business value is implementing prepared concepts and measures. Only through consistency can a value increase be achieved with positive results for the yield. A decisive success factor here is that measures are not only controlled centrally through business control, but all participating employees are involved and made responsible for achieving goals. In practice, the introduction of decentralized control of measures alongside classical controlling has proven useful. The evaluation of the financial effects on yield is the interface between the two systems.

Method

Controlling by degree of implementation is a tool for measuring implementation. This tool categorizes implementation in three phases:

■ Degree 1 of implementation (DI 1). Measures are identified, potentials assessed. All of the concepts and measures to be carried out within the framework of increasing value throughout the business should be assigned to a person who is directly responsible. The possible potentials are estimated using a status-quo analysis and are channelled into the goal definition. Finally, the measures are released by management.

■ Degree 2 of implementation (DI 2). Measures are implemented. Those activities relative to progress are continuously monitored and the results are presented to all stakeholder groups at status meetings.

■ Degree 3 of implementation (DI 3). The effect on yield resulting from these measures is documented. This status has been reached if the yield-relevant potentials have been measured and are reproducible for controlling. In this phase, further steps may need to be taken to achieve the goal.

The advantage of the categorization is that it makes a very detailed perspective of implementation possible (see Figure 7.3). As the potentials in the various degrees of implementation are of differing qualities, this listing of measures provides a realistic perspective of effects on yield. This way, the implementation can be precisely controlled and any deviation corrected. Given, for instance, the fact that potential continuously increases in DI 1 and stagnates in DI 3, it is possible to keep an eye on consistent activities implementation in order to maintain the potentials in DI 3. In the opposite case of stagnating potential constants in DI 1, more focus can be placed on measures and idea creation.

A decisive success factor in the control of measures is the use of decentralized implementation controllers. These controllers direct implementation of measures and activities and are the interface to central direction. The choice of an implementation controller is not, however,

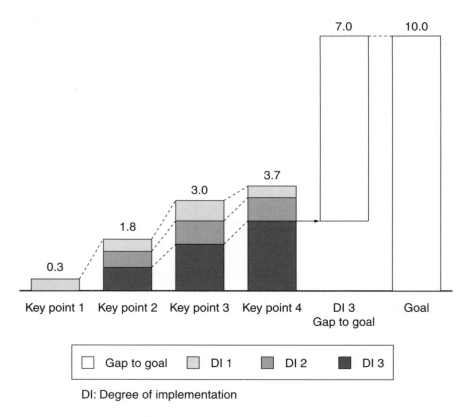

Figure 7.3   Control of measures by degree of implementation

limited to the role of a classic controller from a business background. These implementation controllers are often individuals who possess a fundamental knowledge of strategy and business processes, have a widespread integrated network in the organization, or enjoy the trust of those responsible for measures. It is essential that the measures be followed properly, the methodologies of the implementation phase used correctly and clear reporting paths followed.

Workshop

Together with continuous supervision of measures, workshops can also be conducted within the framework of measures controlling. The goal of this workshop is to use Figure 7.4 to look through the potential evaluations of measures yet again in order to define the following steps for further implementation of these measures. The workshop can also be used to determine those responsible for these measures.

The structure of this workshop can be very pragmatic. It is usually sufficient to go through the ongoing measures in the group, to discuss status, define subsequent steps and adjust the potential evaluation. The results of such workshops are then taken up in the overall status reporting and the new situation evaluated.

Workshop Control of measures							
Perspective/design field	No	Measure	Status	Next step	Responsible	Time point IG3	Requirements
Environment and positioning							
Offer and marketing							
Knowledge and competences							
Value chain and organization							
Measures and controlling							
Leadership and mobilization							
Finance and evaluation							
Opportunities and risk							

Figure 7.4   Workshop: Control of measures

Tip

Setting up a central programme office makes sense in a long-term strategy project. The programme office is a central unit that coordinates the project consistently. It controls and directs the entire programme and reports to management. It also functions as the central hub for the control of measures.

8

Leadership and Mobilizing

Winning over employees

KEY QUESTION

Are targets and motivation systems linked to the strategy?

When a leader sets a goal together with his troops and provides rewards, their spirits are one.

(Sun Tzu)

Management by objectives is an important step in transferring business goals derived from strategy to the operative measures level. This means establishing areas of responsibility, setting goals and determining metrics. Employees and management are involved in this process.

Method

Management initiates the objectives agreement, sets the range and time needed to realize these objectives, communicates strategy and business targets and directs implementation. Employees, together with managers, derive their own targets from the overall target system, coordinate these with strategy and other objectives and then sign off on the agreement.

The starting point for the employee target agreement are the targets set by the BSC. Based on these strategic business targets, the business and the basic question of the direction for the business to develop, together with the relevant levers for achieving this goal (eg opening new markets) are identified. The realization of strategy is implemented at the employee level through the unified setting of metrics (eg sales share of new products, market share in region X) and operative targets. The metrics have the function of providing objective and exact proof of the degree of implementation. It is important to be certain that there is true coherence between what needs to be measured and what is actually measured. The measurement results should be independent of the person measuring them and should be reproducible. Coordinated areas of responsibility are necessary for an objective agreement free of redundant overlap. The area of responsibility describes the results of efforts made by a functional or organizational unit or team (eg sales, customer satisfaction, productivity).

Regarding the consistent implementation of a value based strategy, the setup of the system of management compensation has a decisive role to play. Systems of compensation that have a variable annual component together with a fixed component have long been in use for middle and upper management. Increasingly, approaches are being used that couple the variable portions of compensation to the achievement of previously agreed targets. When defining a value based system of compensation, it is important that it should be a system driven by the customer's market requirements, efforts and behaviour that are directly relevant to achieving the goals set by the strategy. This system also increases yield, is transparent and economically viable. A system of compensation that is strategy oriented is characterized by the following set of advantages:

- A high degree of motivation can be expected because the strategic target of value creation is coupled with the income goals of the manager.

- All decisions and actions in the business are target driven.

- The planning intensity and the plan implementation are promoted. The effect is an increase in yield.

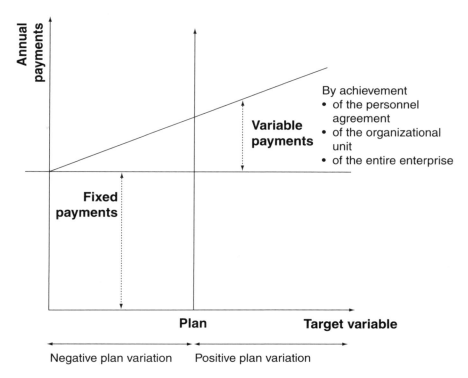

Figure 8.1   Strategy oriented payment system

Workshop

In the workshop, using Figure 8.2, prepare a target agreement for yourself or for discussions with your employees. Which business targets are to be decided on? Which of these can be derived from the BSC and become operative goals for employees? Which measures can be derived? Which further individuals should be involved in order to support the person responsible?

Workshop Employee target agreements				
Business targets	Metrics (derived from the BSC)	Operative targets of the employees	Measures	Responsible

Figure 8.2   Workshop: Employee target agreements

Tip

Note that the objectives agreement is a two-way process in which the creativity of participating individuals can be used to create harmony between business goals and employees. The goal must be to increase both business value from and the market value of an employee. This works especially well when entrepreneurial flexibility is achieved through output oriented target setting.

KEY QUESTION

How can the strategy be embedded in both thought and action?

The spoken word does not carry far enough. Gongs and drums, banners and flags are means whereby the ears and eyes of the host can be focused on one particular point.

(Sun Tzu)

For strategies to be brought to life, they need to be understood, accepted and ultimately implemented by management and personnel. An important tool for the implementation of strategy is targeted communication with employees. It goes almost without saying that personnel need to know the strategy precisely so that they have clear orientation in their everyday work situation. Ensuring that this is the case entails not only the development of information and know-how about the new strategy but also the development of employees' attitudes and behaviour. Through his or her thoughts, actions and behaviour, each individual employee influences the performance of the entire organization. Performance management programmes encompass methods that managers can use to plan, control and improve the performance of personnel in compliance with the higher-level corporate goals. For example, the strategic goal 'customer responsiveness' can only be achieved if all personnel show themselves to be proactive and helpful in relation to their customers. Telephone receptionists will attach particular importance to taking calls promptly and forwarding them in a friendly manner. They realize the contribution they makes to the higher corporate goal and receive direct, consistent feedback relating to their behaviour. The same applies to logistics staff, for example. The drivers are instructed to adopt a helpful approach when delivering goods to customers. These examples demonstrate clearly that strategy is not simply a matter for the upper echelons of management – it must be put into practice by personnel at all levels. The pivotal factor is that the target group is properly informed about the new strategy and the connection between personal sphere of influence and higher corporate objectives is clearly demonstrated. The personnel in question need to understand and accept what the strategy signifies in terms of their everyday work and must know which levers they can impact directly.

Method

To build a holistic performance management programme, it is advisable to use a combination of tools, making due allowance for the specific prerequisites and exigencies of the in-house target groups. A wide range of tools is available to facilitate the continuous implementation of strategies. In Figure 8.3 these tools are positioned in a portfolio on the basis of two dimensions. The 'self-control' dimension indicates the extent to which the target group itself can steer and influence the development and practical implementation of the strategy. The 'level of implementation' dimension shows the degree to which the target group can progress towards implementation as a result of the performance management tool. It is important to note in this context that one-way information is simply not sufficient to convince and/or empower employees to proceed to implementation. The following 'cascade' comes into effect:

■ Thinking is not saying.

■ Saying is not hearing.

■ Hearing is not understanding.

■ Understanding is not being in agreement.

■ Being in agreement is not reaching an agreement.

■ Reaching an agreement is not implementing.

The power of the tools indicated in the portfolio varies in the two dimensions, namely self-control and level of implementation. The range extends from 'pure' information through one-way tools, such as company magazines, to interactive tools, such as business theatre.

In the following section, the key factors for the success of a performance management programme are followed by practical examples to provide the practitioner with specific terms of reference for the configuration of his or her own programmes. The programme was devised by the authors in a major global industrial enterprise with the aim of fostering strategy oriented thought and action in the workforce.

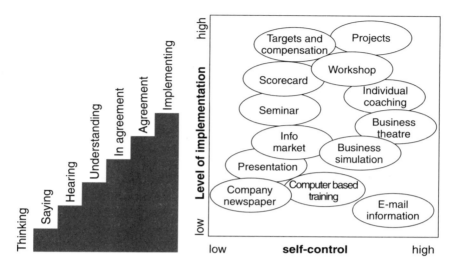

Figure 8.3 Methods of performance management

The following factors are important for the success of implementation.

In-depth analysis of the organization and target group

The first step in the development of a performance management programme is determining the change requirements of personnel on the basis of the company's fundamental future strategic focus. An in-depth analysis of the basic situation, the objectives of the organization and the specific target group ultimately result in the definition of learning, attitude and behavioural goals at employee level that form the framework for overall configuration of the programme.

Example of implementation

The analysis begins with a management workshop designed to clarify the basic operative and strategic situation of the organization. During the one-day event, the current status and the goals of the unit are defined by top management, business unit management, line management and established experts in the organization.

In the course of the workshop, the extent to which the future challenges facing the company necessitate a redefinition of employees' requirement profiles is also examined. The spheres of competence to be developed are derived from the business strategy.

Based on these target profiles, the next step is to carry out a survey among personnel and management for the purpose of analysing skills and competences. The findings of the so-called competence assessment support the identification of gaps in skills and consequently facilitate the definition and prioritization of the principal focus and objectives of the programme.

Development of the programme concept

Developing a business-specific concept for the contents of the programme is of pivotal importance for the success of a performance management programme. The actual process of change begins during this phase with the integration of personnel and management.

Example of implementation

On the basis of a series of 'expert interviews', the contents are harmonized with the organization-specific and business-specific structures and processes. The objectives of the expert interviews include clarification of the business-specific value drivers (eg sales revenue and profit margin targets; cost structures), based on the value driver tree methodology, and identification of the business-specific and function-specific performance drivers (eg in connection with sales and marketing activities and contract and claims management). These performance drivers are matched with the defined business processes and the organization-specific routines are used for the further programme work. The result is the business-specific value driver tree with its actual and projected values. The individual drivers are classified and assigned a binding definition as the basis for execution of the programme.

A number of clusters of performance drivers are formed that experts and management reckon have the greatest relevance for success in a competitive environment. The following have been identified as clusters in the field of sales and marketing, for example: contract management, claim management, risk management, process management and partner management. For these topics, which are of relevance for business success, a number of individual workshop modules are being developed that contain the organization's best practices as well as relevant benchmarks from other enterprises and sectors.

The organization is prepared for the implementation of measures through the integration of management and selected experts and personnel. Final clearance and release of the concept are carried out by the management responsible in the organizational units involved. On the one hand, this ensures support by the entire management team, while on the other hand management is kept informed of the contents and agenda, thus ensuring that these are fully supported during the implementation phase.

The formation of clearly defined target groups (in this example personnel in sales and marketing) ensures that the prerequisites for learning and the transfer of knowledge are homogeneous, eg as a result of sharing the same experience in the same field of work and also as result of common interests and objectives. During the concept development phase it is advisable to integrate process partners (eg project implementation) and to incorporate their views and assessments of the factors that are relevant to ensuring success.

Informing and preparing personnel

The preparatory work, the ambience and the working climate prior to, during and after a measure or activity all have a positive impact on learning motivation and thus on the success of the learning process and performance improvement.

Example of implementation

The purpose of the communication concept is to keep participants informed continually during the entire period of the programme and thus to facilitate control of the execution process. The participants are informed by programme management and top management at regular intervals. Before the programme begins, the participants are provided with an invitation and with initial general information concerning the objectives and contents of the programme. The workshop is presented as a major opportunity for the participants and for the organization as a whole: this in turn gives participants greater motivation to learn and to change.

The invitation is sent out three weeks before the actual event; it contains precise details of the venue, the directions for getting there and the agenda, plus additional information on the next stages planned in connection with the transfer coaching and specific steps for the evaluation of the course. Following each workshop, the results (in the form of electronic documentation) are e-mailed to participants by the moderator. Their superiors are also notified of the results. At the beginning of the programme, the results of the satisfaction survey and the learning achievement are sent at weekly intervals to top management and the other executives involved in the form of a management report. The areas of change (outside the possible influence of participants) determined in the course of the workshop are reported back to management and contacts are established with those persons responsible for implementation.

One week after the workshop, the manager is informed about the employee's participation by programme management and is requested to initiate the implementation coaching. Three months later – halfway through the six-month implementation phase – a survey is carried out among participants to determine the implementation status of their course work and their experience so far in working with the coaches. After a further three months, a final survey is undertaken among the attendees and coaches to determine their assessment of the process and the impact of the results achieved on corporate success. Evaluation of the course work is used to appraise the training scheme with a view to communicating and continually improving the programme.

Form in which content is communicated

The content should be communicated in as clear and practical as manner as possible, ie using examples and relating closely to everyday practice.

Example of implementation

In this example, value driver workshops are held with the personnel. At the beginning of each workshop, information is provided about the agenda and as guidance for the participants. The logical structure of the workshop is outlined and the primary objectives are explained. The agenda for the workshop is visualized as a map: for each unit of the workshop the participants are shown where they currently stand and what goals have been attained so far.

The fact that the workshop is opened by top management not only demonstrates the importance of the programme for the company but also has a highly positive effect on the participants' motivation. At the same time, the straightforward communication of the vision, the concrete objectives and the strategic success factors of the organization establishes a framework for the workshop, emphasizing to participants the relevance of their contribution towards the implementation of strategy.

As a result of the presentation of relevant information and concepts it becomes clear which skills and performance drivers are of decisive importance and how the individual value drivers can be influenced by means of specific courses of action. By working through case studies, the participants can intensify and practice the material they have learned. This is followed by a presentation of the results, with the participants then being supplied with feedback.

At the end of the first day of the workshop the material dealt with in the course of the day is summarized and the participants have an opportunity to review what has been learned and what their expectations are for the remainder of the workshop. During the workshop, repeated references are made to the potential applications of the learning material and their practical use is emphasized. Once the case studies have been dealt with, transfer of the learning material to everyday business is discussed and specific action plans are defined.

A range of different methods and media are employed in the course of the workshop to present information: moderated discussions, tutorials, presentations with overheads and case studies using flipcharts and moderation cards. The use of multiple methods has proven highly effective. The combination of talk or lecture, discussion and exercise with feedback has shown itself to be a particularly effective method.

Use of group work and intensive practising

Practising by oneself improves the long-term effect of learning and thus has a positive long-term impact on personnel's thinking and behaviour.

Example of implementation

Case studies are worked on during the workshop to intensify the learning effect. Cases are dealt with that contain mathematical interrelationships and can be solved with the aid of the information presented in the text. The results are then supplied and appropriate feedback provided.

Another method used is group work, the advantages of which are as follows:

■ The group can do things an individual cannot do.

■ The group is better able to judge.

■ As a general rule, different types of skills, expert knowledge, etc need to be combined in order to solve a particular problem.

■ The ability to learn is better.

■ The 'imaginative ability' is enhanced because the association areas of the members of the group complement one another.

In this example, particular care was taken when forming the groups to achieve a balance between technically and commercially oriented members. This ensured that knowledge owners from the different functions were working together to achieve a successful solution to the task. Prior to the workshop, experienced commercial personnel were identified among the participants and then prepared for their role as experienced contact persons for colleagues with lower levels of know-how.

Care was likewise taken to ensure that a group did not consist of more than five members. Each group was provided with additional background information (eg concerning the factors for successful contract management, claims management, the sales and marketing process), which in turn increased the volume of learning material.

Clear links to relevant business processes and working on your own business

The activity always relates clearly to the business processes and to your own business issues. This can be on the basis of examples of so-called best practice. In addition, participants prepare their own business cases and work on a concrete plan of action during the learning process.

Example of implementation

To increase participants' learning and implementation success, there must be a clearly defined relationship between the learning material and practical uses and applications. The following core questions are dealt with and documented as part of the group work:

- What are the value-related performance drivers that can influence the value drivers (especially costs, cost of capital)?

- What business processes are behind these performance drivers?

- How can we exert a real influence on these performance drivers?

- What obstacles are liable to arise and how can we deal with these?

A member of the group takes responsibility for moderation and documentation of the results.

Role of the consultants

The consultants play a supporting and activating role, helping personnel to identify cause/effect relationships themselves and to work out and apply their own courses of action.

Example of implementation

Consultants and moderators have key responsibility for 'accompanying' participants during the learning and implementation processes. Accordingly, major importance is attached to the choice of suitable trainers and consultants when the course is being put together. The workshop is headed by a team of in-house and external consultants who undergo an assessment and selection process (with final certification) in the run-up to the course.

Management involvement and clear commitment by management

Management provides support during all phases, acting as mentors and coaches.

Example of implementation

Management plays a pivotal role in ensuring the success of the programme. During the analytical and concept development phases, management plots the course ahead and communicates the relevance and the usefulness of the programme. The individual events are opened by representatives of management to provide an overview of the business situation and the future strategic focus of the business unit and also to communicate the expectations and objectives of the workshop.

The workshop is followed by managerial coaching with a view to consolidating transfer of the acquired knowledge and improving overall performance in the working environment.

At the workshop, the participants extract from the learning material three to five concepts that have a personal influence and make a note of these on a special form. The coach is informed about the coachee's participation in the workshop and arranges an initial coaching interview to select and define the learning material (including agreed timetables and targets). The joint definition of goals plays an important role in consolidating the transfer of learning material. The result is a so-called transfer agreement: an agreement on objectives that is signed by both parties. The employee is then responsible for the subsequent implementation of the value enhancement measure. He or she discusses the project with his or her colleagues and project members. Follow-up discussions on the progress and impact of the activity are held with the manager at agreed intervals. The coach provides assistance in connection with any unusual events or problems that occur and supports the coachee during the implementation phase.

The action plans the employee has already prepared during the workshop facilitate the process of goal setting and also the planning of the subsequent implementation stages. It is up to the teams to decide how frequently they hold their meetings. The final session is the only meeting for which a fixed date and time are set. In the parallel evaluation process, continuous feedback about the coaching process and the response of personnel is provided by the organization team.

Measuring success

The success of the measure is gauged in the dimensions 'knowledge', 'attitude' and 'behaviour' and fed back to the organization by way of a systematic dialogue.

Example of implementation

The purpose of programme evaluation is to provide feedback on the impact and progress of the programme. At the same time, the evaluation serves as an integral part of the course, with a powerful learning and learning transfer effect. The evaluation is based on four steps that provide a time structure: reaction, learning / attitude, behaviour and results. The participants are questioned a total of four times at different points over a six-month period.

Course assessment: degree of satisfaction

Participants' satisfaction with the programme is registered by means of a questionnaire that is filled out at the end of the course.

Learning achievement

The level of learning attained is checked by way of 'before and after' tests, the aim being to measure the increase in knowledge that can be directly attributed to the course. Although the 'before' test and the 'after' test have the same structure, in the case of the 'after' test the questions are changed – either partly or completely – to prevent the results being falsified through 'learning by heart'.

Achievement of attitude change

Both self-efficacy and proactivity are registered in order to check 'attitude change'.

Transfer of achievement

Three months after the workshop, a learning transfer survey is carried out among the participants. They are asked to appraise the learning transfer process using a number of scales (eg the implementation status of the agreed measures).

Corporate success – participants and coaches (superiors)

Six months after the workshop and three months after the learning transfer survey, an online questionnaire is sent out to the participants on the one hand and the coaches on the other, in this case the aim being to assess retrospectively whether the goals of the workshop were achieved and what impact the overall course has had on corporate success.

The online questionnaire consists of a total of five parts:

- In the first section, participants are requested to assess the achievement of the individual workshop objectives (the achievement of training goals).

- In the second section, the change in participants' own behaviour is assessed, together with the financial impact of the measures that have been adopted, in order to obtain a company-related evaluation of the changes in employee behaviour (the business impact of the course).

- The third section (on coaching) consists of an overall assessment of the coaching by participants' superior(s) and an appraisal of the barriers to implementation.

- In the fourth section, participants are prompted by open questions to suggest ways in which the programme can be continued and consolidated on a longer-term basis (the next steps).

- In the fifth and final section, both proactivity and self-efficacy are assessed again to estimate the longer-term stability of the attitude-related intervention success of the course.

Workshop

A clearly defined communication concept is the foundation for an effective performance management programme. In the workshop, use Figure 8.4 to draw up the specific communications concept for the implementation of your strategy. What communicative goals are you pursuing? What level on the implementation cascade are you aiming for? What messages are to be communicated and to which target group? Which tools could help you do this? Who is responsible for communication?

Workshop Strategy communication				
What is the goal of the message?	Which stakeholder is this message directed towards?	What is to be communicated?	With which tools?	Who is responsible?

Figure 8.4 Workshop: Strategy communication

Tip

It proves useful in practice to involve the target groups actively in strategy implementation. With this approach, strategies are not imposed on employees without being properly discussed. There should always be ample opportunity to debate the strategy by interactive means. Questions such as 'What exactly does this mean for us?' or 'What obstacles or opportunities do we envisage?' – possibly raised in a workshop – can induce personnel to get involved in implementation and help them identify with the new strategic focus.

9

Finance and Evaluation

Measuring the value of strategy

KEY QUESTION

Does strategy create value?

Measurements, estimates, analyses and comparisons belong to the rules of strategy.

(Sun Tzu)

In recent years, a number of methods have been developed in the area of business valuation. In connection with the expansion of strategy oriented concepts, value oriented business managers are increasingly using the discounted cash flow (DCF) method to determine business value – and, therefore, the value of a given strategy. As a result of the increasing number of business transactions, investment banks, business consultants and the central finance departments of companies have started to use the DCF method. By using this method, the marginal price for a business (value of equity) is determined as the difference between the value for the entire business minus the value of debt. This method can be used to evaluate expected business development. In realizing the strategy, the derivable financial index variable controls the success of its implementation over time.

Method

The business value is calculated by discounting the free cash flows that are available for payment to shareholders and outside lenders of the business with the average cost of capital of the business. Because indirect abstraction of business value is through the total business value, this approach is known as the entity method. The DCF method, as an evaluation model, is basically carried out in four stages.

Stage 1: Determination of the free cash flow

First, the free cash flow for each period within the planning horizon is calculated using the following formula. The free cash flows to be expected in the future are, as a rule, determined retroactively from the planned profit/loss calculation of the business itself, the content of which is derived from the strategic plan that results from the derived operational measures.

The free cash flow thus calculated shows – in the case of a negative amount – the financing requirements. In the case of a positive amount, it is the surplus available for dividends, interest and amortization.

	Earnings before interest and tax (EBIT)
x	(1 – marginal tax rate)
=	**Earnings after tax**
+	Depreciation
=	**Gross cash flow**
+/–	Reduction or growth of net working capital*
–	Expenses for investment in business assets
+/–	Change in other assets
=	**Operating free cash flow**
+/–	Non-operating cash flow
=	**Free cash flow (FCF)**

* Net working capital = current assets minus current liabilities

Stage 2: Determining the cost of capital

To calculate the total business value in stage 3, it is necessary to calculate a cost of capital that adequately covers the risks. When one takes into account that systems of taxation in general are not, for instance, neutral regarding financing due to the fact that interest on debt can usually be deducted from taxes, the type of capital structure chosen by management has a considerable influence on the value of the business. The cost of financing can be derived comparatively easily from the yield on bonds or bank liabilities. The tax benefits of using debt is calculated by multiplying the interest on debt by the factor 1 (the marginal tax rate). The return on equity is obtained by using the capital asset pricing model (CAPM). According to this model, the anticipated return on equity is the risk-free rate of interest added to a business specific, weighted, market risk premium. The total cost of capital is calculated on this basis as the weighted average of the anticipated returns on equity and debt. The desired shares of the market value pertaining to equity and debt, relative to the total market value of capital, are taken as the weighting factors. It is important to use the market value of the firm's equity and debt and not the balance sheet values. Calculating values based on non-existent data is a problem. The reason for this is that these values can only be calculated if the weighted average cost of capital (WACC) is known. To solve this problem in practice, a projected capital structure is referenced, which management sets for the business instead of the actual existing capital structure.

Equity cost of capital
(according to the capital asset pricing model: CAPM)
r_e: Anticipated return on equity
r_f: Risk-free rate of interest
r_m: Anticipated return on market portfolio
BETA:
Measure of business specific risk

$$r_e = r_f + BETA*(r_m - r_f)$$

Debt cost of capital
r_d: Interest on debt
T_c: Marginal tax rate of the company

$$r_d \text{ after tax} = r_d \text{ before tax} * (1-Tc)$$

Weighted average cost of capital (WACC)
MVE: Market value of equity
MVD: Market value of debt
TMV: Total market value

$$WACC = [MVE/TMV] * r_e + [MVD/TMV]*r_d \text{ after tax}$$

Stage 3: Determining the total market value of the company (business value)

The free cash flow for each period is discounted with the WACC. The resulting current value can then be added, thus producing the total business value (BV).

Total Business Value (BV)	$BV = \Sigma \, [FCF_{t/}(1 + WACC)^t]$

Stage 4: Determining the value of the firm's equity.

The value of the firm's equity is calculated by deducting its debt from the total business value.

Equity value (EV)	$EV = BV - MVD = \Sigma \, [FCF_{t/}(1 + WACC)^t] - MVD$

Like any future oriented evaluation, the DCF method requires a forecast of the free cash flow. This is derived from the strategic plan operative measures based on the strategic plan to be carried out. Within the planning horizon, an attempt is made to estimate the free cash flow as precisely as possible for each year. Looking at the end of the planning horizon, for the sake of simplicity, a constant value is then chosen to be used as a 'going concern value'. This calculated value can be taken as a discounted perpetual return for the average periodic free cash flows that are anticipated in the distant future (after the end of the planning horizon).

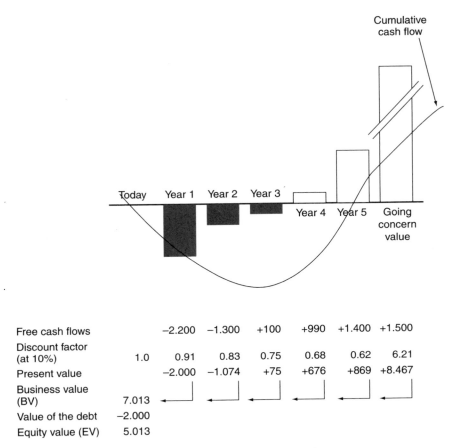

Figure 9.1 Company valuation by the DCF method

Workshop

You have developed concrete measures and an implementation plan on the basis of all previous considerations in your strategy. In a workshop, you can now evaluate what impact the measures have on the cash flow during which periods (see Figure 9.2). In order to find plausible plan values, you have to make a series of assumptions. Practice has shown that this requires a certain degree of courage because these values are really only planning values and not exact, predictable values. A plausible framework of assumptions can, however, provide a corridor of values within which the value of the strategy is likely to range.

Workshop Financial plan and evaluation								
	Today	Year 1	Year 2	Year 3	Year 4	Year 5	Future
(I) Cash inflow								
(II) Cash outflow								
(III) = Free cash flows								
(IV) Surplus (derived from cumulative (III))								
(V) Present values (discounted from (III))								
(VI) Business value (derived from sum (V))								

Figure 9.2   Workshop: Financial plan and evaluation

Tip

It is helpful to set up the evaluation model using computer based worksheets. The individual variables in the DCF can thus be analysed relative to their influence on the value of the firm's equity. In the case of variables with an especially strong influence, it is necessary to check whether the assumptions in the strategic plan are consistent and which further measures need to be considered to achieve value enhancement.

10

Opportunities and Risks

Managing uncertainty

KEY QUESTION

How can risks be changed into opportunities?

The considerations of the wise always take into account both the usefulness and the damage. Because they weigh the usefulness, their work can grow. Because they weigh the damage, their problems can be overcome.

(Sun Tzu)

Businesses carry a variety of risks. Some of these risks are centred on the business model itself (production risks), whereas other parts of the business are affected by external risks that have no direct connection with value creation in the original sense (currency fluctuations, for instance). All factors that have a negative influence on business value may be considered to be risks and there is invariably a feeling that they might arise unexpectedly.

From a strategic point of view, the term risk is not limited to negative influences but also encompasses a suboptimal development of recognized strategic opportunities and defined possibilities for development. The amount of risk to be expected by the business also has an effect on the amount of shareholder equity and the external capital interest rate. The greater the risk to be anticipated, and thus the fluctuations in the profit, the greater the expenses for the cost of capital to be factored in. Allowance must be made for the fact that every business has only a limited ability to bear risk on its own. This ability to bear risk depends, among other things, on whether the equity necessary to assure survival provides an adequate buffer if a problem arises. The smaller the buffer against risk provided by equity and the greater the risks, the greater the interest requirements of external capital providers. To ensure the potential for the success of the strategy appropriately, risk management is necessary that identifies the risks, evaluates them, takes adequate measures to counter them, and is strictly applied to the strategy implementation.

Method

Risk management as a business assessment concept aims at lowering the probability that a problem will occur or at least reducing the potentially negative influence of such a problem on the business. The cycle of risk management has four stages.

Risk identification

Regarding the possible causes of risk, it is useful to initially classify them under the categories of environmental risks, operative risks and credit risks:

- Environmental risks can result from discontinuities and trends in the macro-economic environment as well as from the action of competitive forces in a sector. The instruments of environmental and competitive analysis presented here are suitable to identify these risks. The status quo and changes in politics and law, in the behaviour of competitors, in technological developments and in customer preferences can be examined in greater detail.

- Operative risks result from the specific design of the value creation chain, the relationships to suppliers, together with the necessary establishment and maintenance of core competences. The starting point for the identification of operative risks should, therefore, be the business model. This has been explicitly defined in the strategy, as have the value drivers allocated to the business model. Additionally, the incidental risks arising from technical failure, human error or acts of God must be taken into account.

■ Credit risks include the possibility that a debtor does not meet a just and due request for payment or that the debtor's creditworthiness declines.

The system of risk categories can be further broken down in its structure. This procedure supports the most comprehensive identification of the risks possible, creates a business-wide basis for risk oriented communication and makes possible the aggregation of risks throughout the organization.

Risk evaluation

The identified risks are evaluated in the second step with regard to the probability of their occurrence and their possible impact on business value (in this context, economic value added). In this step, the possible influences on sales, operative expenses, business assets and cost of capital are quantified. On the basis of this evaluation, priorities for the next steps in risk management can be worked out.

Risk handling

Regarding effective and efficient risk handling, diverse points of attack can be considered:

■ The strategy of risk avoidance can be applied to risks that have a high probability of occurring and/or have considerable potential for influencing business value. The central question here is: does the profit gained by taking the risk justify the size of the risk? It may, for instance, very well make sense to avoid an especially high risk that results from a certain customer order by simply not accepting the order.

■ Selective risk diversification is achieved by distributing various risks. These strategies may use investment banking in the design of the risk structure for their assets.

■ The sale of risks to insurance firms can prevent business losses through fire or in the case of liability claims against the business.

■ For reduction of risk or reduction of claims, interest and currency fluctuations the capital market provides the tools of factoring and risk hedging.

■ A risk transfer to various stakeholder groups can be carried out. This may be performed with customers, suppliers, outside capital lenders or government.

Risk control

Once all the possibilities of risk management have been exhausted, a residual risk remains that must be rigorously controlled. The cycle of risk management is closed by risk control.

The following points are critical to success:

■ Risk management must be anchored in both the structural and process organization. This means the role of management must be clearly defined (eg taking complete responsibility in accordance with legal requirements). This includes, where applicable, a team of experts set up especially for risk management (eg involved in development and training of risk management methods).

■ The basis for risk control is the presence of a systematic process for identifying risks. Only in this way is it possible to be assured that risks can be identified through the functional and responsible areas of the business.

■ Setting up responsible person based reporting, a clear assignment of responsibility for specific risks, and agreeing on concrete goals relative to the implementation of those measures for managing risk are all important factors.

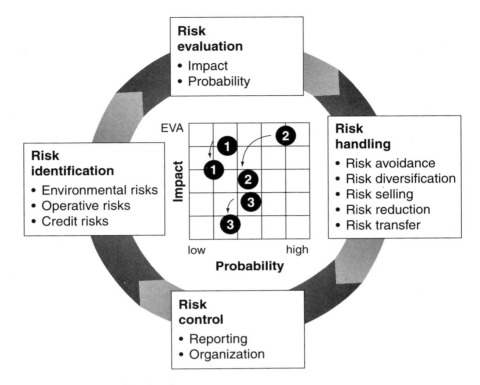

Figure 10.1   Cycle of risk management

(source: Wittmann/Reuter/Magerl (2007), p.136)

Workshop

Workshops conducted periodically are excellent for setting up and implementing sustainable risk management (see Figure 10.2). At the same time, measures aimed at risk identification, risk evaluation, risk handling and risk control can be carried out.

Workshop Risk management					
What risks can be identified?	Risk evaluation		Risk evaluation	Status of implementation	Responsible
	Impact	Probability			

Figure 10.2   Workshop: Risk management

Tip

In the preparation of a workshop on risk management, a structured interview of experts can be of use. Selected managers and employees from various functional areas can provide valuable input, resulting in the most thorough risk identification possible, together with an evaluation of the risks in all risk categories. Additionally, their creative potential can be used to gather effective suggestions for managing risk.

In challenging projects or in businesses subject to extremely rapid changes in the environment, workshops on risk management are consequently to be anchored and the cycle for carrying them out should be relatively short (eg weekly). Participants thus always bear the risk perspective in mind, permitting them to recognize impending risks at an early stage and to take the appropriate countermeasures.

11

Conclusion
Keeping the essentials in focus

Conclusion – What does Sun Tzu have to say?

The ancient Chinese Master Sun Tzu has accompanied us throughout our journey with timeless items of wisdom from his classic *The Art of War*. These ideas were formulated more than 2000 years ago, yet, as we have observed again and again, they remain as relevant today as the day he wrote them down. We are fully convinced that these central aspects are still important in today's world. Sun Tzu's work is the basis for successful strategic management. He has shown us that strategy is to be understood as discipline, one in which relationships and energy take centre stage. The seeming paradox in Sun Tzu's work is the rejection of direct enemy engagement. This superior strategy proves itself, according to Sun Tzu, because it prepares actively for the future.

> *He who does not fight is truly victorious.*
> *The great things in the world must be done while they are still small.*
> *For this reason, the wise never do that which is great and this is the reason why they achieve such greatness.*
>
> (Sun Tzu, *The Art of War*)

We would do well to heed his teachings!

Appendix
Case study – EasyLife GmbH

EASYLIFE

A case study on strategy and business planning

This case study was specifically developed for discussion on the subject of strategy and business planning. The contents of the case study are entirely imaginary. Any resemblance to existing enterprises is unintentional and purely coincidental.

The case study is intended to assist:

- executives who need to reorient an existing business in a new competitive field;

- successors of entrepreneurs who need to develop and implement for the continued success of an existing business;

- executives with corporate responsibility ('intrapreneurs') who are responsible for developing their business unit strategically and operationally;

- innovators and their teams who drive products, process and market innovations in a young, developing organization;

■ consultants who support entrepreneurs and their teams in value oriented business development.

In this case study you are in the role of a consultant in the field of strategy and business planning at Sombrero Strategy Consulting (SSC). Through the four phases of the strategic management process (analysis, conception, implementation and controlling) you will coach your customer, EasyLife GmbH, a company in the white goods market. EasyLife GmbH is currently facing the challenges of a new strategic positioning of its business, setting up an innovative strategy for value creation and long-term success.

The main partners in this case study are:

■ management at Sombrero Strategy Consulting (SSC):
   – Jean-Paul Vutour: Director, Sombrero Strategy Consulting (SSC)
   – Sian Hang: Project Management, SSC 'Strategy at EasyLife'

■ management at EasyLife GmbH:
   – Dr Achim Junick: Managing Director, EasyLife GmbH
   – Professor Elke R Forsch: Head of Corporate Project 'Strategy at EasyLife'.

Phase I: Analysis

Jean-Paul Vutour
From: <jeanpaul.vutour@Sombrero.com>
To: <sian.hang@Sombrero.com>
Sent: Wednesday 24 October 2010, 16:17
Insert: easylife_profile.pdf
Subject: Canvassing for consulting project at EasyLife GmbH

Dear Sian,

I told you not long ago that I got to know Dr Achim Junick, the Managing Director of EasyLife GmbH, at a golf tournament for businesspeople in Marienhof. He only took over the management post in January and is currently in the process of giving the company a completely new strategic focus. As the *Financial Times* reported recently in an article, he has decided to put 'trendsetting strategic innovation' high on his corporate agenda and hopes to secure a considerable edge over his competitors in this field within the foreseeable future.

He took the opportunity to talk to me about the performance of Sombrero shares since the introduction of the company's 'strategic innovation' programme five years ago. This gave me a chance to draw his attention to the service portfolio of our Sombrero Strategy Consulting unit. He wasn't aware that we use our knowledge base in the field of strategic management to provide consulting not only internally but also externally for selected partners. Since Sombrero has built up a promising strategic partnership with EasyLife over the past few years, our managing board takes the view that there's nothing to stop a transfer of know-how in this case.

I have met Achim Junick again since then. He is very interested in 'participating in our experience curve' and possibly in giving us a consulting assignment for strategic management. I told him I would pass this important project on to you, since you and your people in our team probably have the widest experience in this sector, with you having been both an strategic manager and a senior consultant.

I have arranged a further meeting with Dr Junick for Friday 3 December 2010 to discuss the terms of a possible order more specifically. There are one or two matters you could help me with as I prepare for this next meeting.

Assignment 1: Innovation practice: I am requesting you to hold a workshop, together with our innovation experts team, which will focus on our Sombrero experience in relation to the following question: Which aspects of corporate strategy and culture have a positive/negative effect on an enterprise's efforts to position itself as an 'strategic innovation trendsetter'?

Assignment 2: Key success factors: Which key success factors can we derive from this for a potential innovation strategy and culture project entitled 'Strategic innovation at EasyLife'?

You will find attached a brief analysis of the company, which our competitor research department has compiled on EasyLife GmbH and which I am using as I prepare for the next meeting.

Sincerely yours,

Jean-Paul

Jean Paul Vutour
Director Sombrero Strategy Consulting (SSC)
St.-Martin-Strasse 76
81541 München
Germany
Attachment: easylife_profile.pdf

Company profile of EasyLife GmbH (Group)
(Status: October 2010)

General information and SWOT analysis

Company headquarters	Düsseldorf
CEO	Dr. Achim Junick
No. of employees (worldwide)	31,452 including: 30% in Western Europe, 43% in Germany, 7% in Eastern Europe, 4% in North America, 7% in Latin America, 9% in Asia
No. of manufacturing plants	32
No. of subsidiaries	49
Customers	All over the world, customers regard the EasyLife brands as being synonymous with innovative technology, outstanding design and top quality. Purchasing decisions centre on the following four factors: • high degree of efficiency and performance • high degree of convenience and user friendliness • intelligent technology • environmental friendliness. It should also be pointed out that requirements vary substantially in the different regional markets.
Management/human resources	• EasyLife views its corporate culture as a global network based on an open dialogue between different sets of people in different cultures. In practice, however, certain gaps in this culture are evident from time to time. The primary corporate values are considered to be mutual respect, fairness in interpersonal dealings and management which is based on partnership and motivation.

- In most cases, managerial posts are filled by personnel from within the organization. Those who are ready and willing to develop their specialist and interpersonal skills have every opportunity to do so. Over the past few years, the concept of 'entrepreneurs in an enterprise' has become an integral part of the managerial culture.
- Personnel often describe EasyLife's structure as being 'hierarchical'.

Product range

Full range of household appliances: washing machines, dryers, cookers, dishwashers, refrigerators, deep freezes, floor polishers.

easylife_profile.pdf

Strengths	• Introduction of a value based management model as its pivotal managerial philosophy and as a basis for the payment of top management (this was implemented in 2005).
	• The brand is associated with a very positive quality image.
	• International network of affiliated companies.
	• The production facilities and the sales and marketing organization have followed the global strategic focus.
	• Ecological auditing throughout the product lifecycle and development of environmentally friendly products.
Weaknesses Comparative weaknesses in innovation management* *according to a benchmarking study undertaken by the McKinley consulting company (comparison with principal competitors)	• No clear positioning in terms of competitive strategy.
	• Recurring problems with time to market.
	• Loss of key customers last year (see sales).
	• Innovations are incremental rather than radical (trendsetting).
	• Insufficient compatibility in the international and intercontinental innovation processes.
	• Diversified (partly incompatible) IT structure.
	• Innovations are not geared adequately to segment-specific customer requirements.
	• In many cases, lack of innovation incentives for personnel below the top management echelon.
	• Only German Centres of Competence.
	• No internal venture capital available.
	• Hardly any incentives for the development of a culture of innovation.
	• The potential for customer retention and innovation in the customer service and after-sales management sectors is not utilized to the full.

Opportunities
Probable
developments in the
domestic appliance
sector

- Continued stagnation in Germany – still no impetus from ongoing tax reforms.
- Global economic recovery shows a continuing upward trend.
- The dollar exchange rate is making the United States more competitive.
- Interest rates reach an historic low in the United States – this has a knock-on effect globally and a positive impact on economic revival.
- There are positive sales expectations for Asia, Eastern Europe and North America.
- Further economic trends: political risks, more restrictive policies in the public sector, tight money and financial policies, major increase in the price of energy and raw materials, rise in the value of the euro.

Threats
Risks according to
status report

- EU directives on the return and recycling of electrical and electronic refrigeration appliances (since 2003) are a model for other regions.
- Restrictions on specific hazardous substances in electrical and electronic appliances are anticipated not only in the EU but also in other countries (United States, certain Asian countries).
- Interest and currency exchange risks.
- Economic risks are still expected in Brazil and Argentina.
- The international trend towards the restructuring of social security systems is curbing consumer demand and impacting cost structures in the group's local companies.
- Overcapacities in the household appliance sector.
- Greater market saturation and increasing price wars in the industry.
- Overall picture: no sign of risks that could threaten the firm's existence at present.

Financial situation

Sales revenues by region	2015 (strategic plan)	2009 (actual status)
	Germany: 20% Rest of Western Europe: 32% Eastern Europe: 10% North America: 5% Latin America: 5% Asia: 27% Miscellaneous: 1%	Germany: 26% Rest of Western Europe: 54% Eastern Europe: 6% North America: 5% Latin America: 3% Asia: 5% Miscellaneous: 1%

Overview of financial data (several years)	2009	2008	2007	2006
Net sales (in millions of €)	4,860	4,995	5,039	5,336
Employees (in thousands on reporting date)	31.5	31.9	32.0	32.2
Personnel costs	1,125	1,100	1,091	1,098
Investment in property, plant and equipment (as % of net sales)	3.3	2.9	2.8	3.1
Depreciation on property, plant and equipment (as % of investment)	102	104	89	110
Total assets (in millions of €)	3,251	3,166	3,101	3,096
Shareholders' equity (as % of total assets)	25	23	22	18
Accrued liabilities (in millions of €)	1,133	998	855	811
Earnings before interest and tax (in millions of €)	122	149	201	133
Research and development (as % of total expenditure)	1.4	1.3	2.1	1.8

Phase II: Conception

Dr Achim Junick
From: <achim.junick@easylife.com>
To: <jeanpaul.vutour@Sombrero.com>;<sian.hang@Sombrero.com>
cc: <elke.forsch@easylife.com>
Sent: Monday 6 December 2010, 9:05
Subject: Project innovation strategy at EasyLife

Dear Mr Vutour,
Dear Mr Hang,

I would like to begin by thanking you again for your team's excellent presentation of Sombrero's experience in the field of strategic innovation management. What pleased me particularly was that we were able to identify the initial ideas for the corporate project 'Innovation strategy at EasyLife' during our joint discussions. I was also highly impressed by your consulting philosophy of 'process accompaniment'. I believe this is the right approach to furthering and focusing our company's many ideas and considerable experience in the field of innovation strategy and also raising them to a sustainably competitive level on the basis of the experience you have gained at Sombrero.

As discussed, I am now placing with you an order for the initial project phase in accordance with the terms and conditions you outlined. This phase is scheduled to be completed by the end of February next year. The objective is to strengthen EasyLife's strategic position and its innovative flair and to develop and anchor the success factors for innovation strategy and culture already referred to.

Immediately after our meeting on Friday, I discussed the ideas with Professor Elke Forsch, the head of our Research and Development Centre in Bad Neustadt. She, too, was highly impressed by the ideas and concepts. As a result, we agreed on Friday that she will take over responsibility for our 'Innovation strategy at EasyLife' programme immediately.

So that we can get off to a smooth start in January, we should launch the project officially in December. I welcome the idea of forming a steering committee in which you, Mr Vutour and myself make decisions on future courses of action. I have requested Ms Forsch to get in touch with Mr Hang directly. Ms Forsch will also be sending you, as mentioned, the market research findings on developments in the white goods market.

I look forward to working with you on this highly promising project.

Sincerely yours,

Achim Junick
Dr Achim Junick
Managing Director EasyLife GmbH
EasyLife Group Head Office
Düsseldorf
Germany

Elke R Forsch
From: <elke.forsch@easylife.com>
To: <sian.hang@Sombrero.com>
cc: <jeanpaul.vutour@Sombrero.com>; <achim.junick@easylife.com>;
Sent: Monday 6 December 2010, 10:15
Insert: WhiteGoodsMarket.doc
Subject: Initial preparatory meeting

Dear Mr Hang,

As you will no doubt have heard from Dr Junick, I took over
responsibility for our corporate project 'Innovation strategy at
EasyLife' last Friday. I propose that we get together for an initial
meeting some time this week. Would Thursday 9 December be
suitable? I suggest we meet here at the R&D Centre in Bad
Neustadt. Please let me know if that is OK with you.

You will find enclosed a brief analysis of the white goods market
and our main competitors. The principal focus is on after-sales
service, support from internet platforms, and a number of key
trends affecting the industry. This should provide us with our first
overview of the competitive challenges we face.

Best regards,

Elke Forsch

Professor Elke R. Forsch
Head of R&D Centre
EasyLife GmbH
Bad Neustadt
Germany
Attachment: WhiteGoodsMarket.doc

File: WhiteGoodsMarket.doc

Research topic: Services in the white goods market

Industry: Household appliances and consumer goods
Content: Benchmarking on: after-sales service, internet
             platforms/support, new developments
Sources: Euromonitor, Frost & Sullivan, Datamonitor, Gartner
             Group, international press releases

After-sales service

In 2009, manufacturers and retailers increased their focus on after-sales service as a marketing tool to attract consumers and to induce them to purchase higher priced or more complex products. After-sales service, especially warranties and repair agreements, helps to compensate for the risk customers feel they take when purchasing technologically advanced products. The key areas of after-sales service that manufacturers focus on include:

- price guarantees, with refunds offered if the same product is on sale at a lower price elsewhere;
- performance guaranteed, covering specifics such as foods damaged by faulty refrigerators;
- special financial deals, such as credit facilities or leasing;
- free/low-price installation/delivery/servicing/repairs;
- removal and safe disposal of old appliances;
- internet based technical support, especially for advanced technology and computerized appliances;
- toll-free service hotlines and remote diagnosis to save repair costs;
- longer warranties to gain customer trust and acquire more detailed information about customers.

Internet platforms/support

Manufacturers are generally reluctant to sell their goods directly via the internet for fear of disrupting delicate relationships with their traditional distributors. Consumers use the websites of suppliers primarily as a source of information and prefer to purchase products through a traditional retailer. Some companies are keen on improving quality and facilitating communication through the use of internet applications and by setting up service platforms (eg Songsung and Latsushita in Asia).

General Comfort's website allows parts orders and online searches for models.

Three of the world's largest suppliers of kitchen appliances are setting up a pan-European electronic trading venture. Under the scheme, retailers are able to access lists of products and check details such as price and availability. Transactions will be made on the basis of secure communications paths. The firms involved in this venture are Electrofox, Whirltool, General Comfort and EasyLife.

New developments in the networked home area

The major new trend in the large kitchen appliances sector is the development of networked appliances connected to one other and to external facilities, including after-sales service and the internet. Most leading manufacturers have invested in research in this field and have established partnerships with specialist companies with a view to developing connectivity protocols, ie the creation of networked appliances with companies that are able to provide connectivity for the appliances themselves. This includes broadband internet access, a residential gateway and networking technology to provide the connectivity between appliances. Here are some examples:

- The latest innovation in refrigeration appliances is the emergence of intelligent refrigerators, creating a super premium category. Most major manufacturers have invested in the development of internet-enabled fridge freezers, although such products are not yet widely available. Intelligent refrigerators, which are connected to other home appliances as well as to the internet and to the 'outside world', offer considerable potential for added convenience. Possible functions include remote diagnostics, energy savings, detection of low food supplies, and direct placement of orders with the supermarket.
- Internet-equipped laundry appliances were also introduced toward the end of the review period, including Songsung's 'White Knight': these appliances can be networked with other

household appliances, are compatible with remote diagnostics, and can be programmed to start at specific times.
- Microwaves with internet-enabled modules include preprogrammed and customizable recipes.

Benchmarking

The Gartner Group published the following benchmarking survey, which provides an overview of the current position/anticipated development of rankings (June 2010) of major competitors in the white goods market.

Company	After-sales service	Internet platforms/ support	Networked appliances	Forecast development of future ranking/comment on latest developments
Arcethink	↓	↓	↕	↘ Initiated home information infrastructure project in R&D
EasyLife	↓	↑	↕	↗ Expansion of customer service and parts supplier networks
Electrofox	↑	↕	↕	→ Restructuring and focus on digitization and networks
General Comfort	↑	↑	↑	↗ Joint venture with Loricson to develop smart home products
Latsushita	↑	↕	↑	↗ Linked with Microloft to create smart home appliances based on the Universal Plug & Play Protocol
Maroni	↕	↕	↕	→ Home solutions initiative programme
Songsung	↕	↑	↑	↗ Home information infrastructure project to link together major household appliances
Whirltool	↕	↓	↕	↘ Negotiating with Songsung concerning potential takeover

↑   Top position in industry (among the top three competitors)
↕   Industry average
↓   Follower ranking
→↗↘ Expected competitive improvements in ranking (steady-state, gain, loss)

Sian Hang
From: <sian.hang@Sombrero.com>
To: <elke.forsch@easylife.com>
cc: <jeanpaul.vutour@Sombrero.com>; <achim.junick@easylife.com>;
    < innovationsteam@easylife.com>
Sent: Wednesday 15 December 2010, 11:22
Insert: innovationsprocess.pdf
Subject: Phase: Conception of strategy

Dear Elke,

What a brilliant kickoff meeting that was on Monday with the joint team – highly effective and at such short notice. I am sending you as an attachment an overview of the strategy process (Level 0), the design of which we will be using (and modifying) as the basis for our 'Innovation strategy at EasyLife' project.

I also welcome the fact that we will be holding the next workshop with the team right at the beginning of the New Year (as agreed: Friday/Saturday 14/15 January 2011). I have been in touch with our hotel management people in the meantime and arranged a venue that will be ideal for our workshop at which we hope to create a 'picture of the future'. Just wait and see…!

Here again a brief summary of the different points we will be dealing with at the workshop.

Assignment 3: Analyse trends in external environment. The first stage will be to examine the main structural trends for the next 5 to 10 years using the so-called PESTEL method of analysis. We have used this tool with considerable success, especially since it provides a holistic view of the business environment. We will be taking a close look at trends in the political, economic, socio-cultural, ecological and legal environments. I have no doubt that it will give us a powerful strategic framework for our future course of action.

Assignment 4: 'Picture of the future'. The second stage will take us into the future: using our so-called 'pictures of the future' method (in short: 'PoF' – everything has to be abbreviated at Sombrero!) and on the basis of the environmental analytics referred to above, we will be developing a picture of possible future applications – hopefully with a large measure of creativity. In our view, the creation of convincing pictures that are in line with customer preferences and technical capabilities is a basic prerequisite for lasting success and goal-oriented innovations. We should describe our ideas on the basis of the fulfillment of customer requirements and the possible features.

Assignment 5: Trendsetting innovations. Using our PoF as a basis, we will then work out and describe a number of trendsetting innovations. The objective here is to try and take a much broader view of things. We call this approach 'radical' because it may well mean breaking with existing conventions. We should be aware that the innovation potential may refer to products, services and new business models.

Just one more question: who do you think we should add to the group of participants? Experience has shown that very often the best ideas come from 'lateral thinkers' and other outsiders...

Our motto must be 'Creating value by creativity'! I'm really looking forward to getting down to work on this highly interesting process.

Sincerely yours,

Sian

Dr Achim Junick
From: <achim.junick@easylife.com>
To: <elke.forsch@easylife.com>
cc: <jeanpaul.vutour@Sombrero.com>;
   <sian.hang@Sombrero.com> <innovationsteam@easylife.com>
Sent: Monday 24 January 2011, 11:30
Subject: 1st steering committee project 'Innovation strategy at
     EasyLife'

Dear Ms Forsch,

I would like to refer again briefly to the first meeting of our steering committee yesterday afternoon.

In my opinion, the ideas presented in connection with 'pictures of the future' and the actual concepts for trendsetting innovations were excellent. We have now reached a point, however, at which we need to think carefully about what we are going to focus on with our limited resources. Because of the current liquidity squeeze we have to depend on the support of investors for the development of innovative sectors, with the result that we need a clear assessment method on the basis of which we can reach a decision concerning our priorities. Accordingly, I would like to entrust the following task to the team – to be completed by our next steering committee meeting at the end of February:

Assignment 6: Evaluation criteria. Please draw up a catalogue of relevant idea evaluation criteria that we can use in order to prioritize and select strategic innovations at EasyLife in the future.

I suggest that at the next meeting of the steering committee we take a closer look at the innovation that receives highest priority. Any proposal you have about this would be welcome.

Assignment 7: Description of the innovation ideas based on the structure of a business plan. Please draw up a more detailed description for the highest priority innovation, dealing with the key aspects of the idea briefly but at the same time comprehensively – rather in the manner of an executive summary for venture capital. In other words, I would like to have a clear picture of the target group, the type of solution proposed for the problem, the technologies and competences required, the value chain requirements, the milestones, the chief 'value creation' levers, and an overview of the greatest risks that might arise from the roadmap.

According to the project plan, the first project phase that has been commissioned will have been reached by the time of the second meeting of the steering committee. I would then like to decide how we should move ahead into a possible next phase and whether we should enlist the services of Sombrero Strategy Consulting for that as well.

Sincerely yours,
Achim Junick
Dr Achim Junick
Managing Director EasyLife GmbH
EasyLife Group Head Office

Phase III: Implementation

Sian Hang
From: <sian.hang@Sombrero.com>
To: <elke.forsch@easylife.com>
Sent: Monday 24 January 2011, 22:10
Subject: Idea-buy-in for innovations

Dear Elke,

Today's e-mail from Dr Junick has again demonstrated that it is not enough to develop good ideas – we also need to 'sell' them. In short:

> Thought does not mean said
> Said does not mean heard
> Heard does not mean understood
> Understood does not mean agreed
> Agreed does not mean implemented – not by a long way!

The following idea came to me in this connection. In the next stage we have to win over very different target groups for our innovation idea: our internal management, investors, internal partners within the organization and – first and foremost – our customers, of course! I suggest therefore that the next stage should be a so-called 'idea buy-in'. This is how it would work:

Assignment 8: Stakeholders' expectations. First of all we need to focus on the expectations of our 'stakeholders', the partners referred to above. What do they expect? How can we win them over? What factors for success can we work out in order to actually achieve an 'idea buy-in'?

Assignment 9: Preparation of a presentation for stakeholders. On this basis we should prepare a presentation, which should then be given an internal dry run. This will give us a greater sense of security and will allow us to take a long hard look at the dos and don'ts.

Assignment 10: Setting up the performance management programme. Which additional measures can be launched to win over the employees for successful implementation of the strategy?

What's your view?

Sian

Elke R Forsch
From: <elke.forsch@easylife.com>
To: <sian.hang@Sombrero.com>
cc: <innovationsteam@easylife.com>
Sent: Monday 24 January 2011, 23:15
Subject: (Re): Idea buy-in for innovations

Dear Sian,

I like your idea of the inhouse dry run. That's how we'll do it! Let's start with that at our next meeting on Wednesday. I've put the whole team in the 'cc'. Please take charge of the briefing in the workshop.

Regards,

Elke

Elke R. Forsch
From: <elke.forsch@easylife.com>
To: <sian.hang@Sombrero.com>; <innovationsteam@easylife.com>
Sent: Thursday January 27 2011, 9:55
Subject: Idea buy-in for innovations

Dear members of the team,

Earlier than originally planned, we now have the opportunity to give the presentation on innovation.

I am again expecting significant input from the feedback from the meetings. I feel that after this week's efforts we are excellently prepared for Monday.

Would everyone who is giving a presentation please come to my office at 2.00 pm today for coordinating discussions, so that we can clarify the final details and decide who will collect the feedback points at the meetings?

Kind regards,

Elke Forsch

Professor Elke R Forsch
Head of R&D Centre
EasyLife GmbH
Bad Neustadt
Germany

Phase IV: Controlling

Dr Achim Junick
From: <achim.junick@easylife.com>
To: <jeanpaul.vutour@Sombrero.com>; <sian.hang@Sombrero.com>
cc: <elke.forsch@easylife.com
Sent: Friday 25 February 2011, 9:01
Subject: Project: Strategic innovation at EasyLife

Dear Mr Vutour,
Dear Mr Hang,

I would like to thank you very much for the extremely professional support during the initial phase of the 'Strategic innovation at EasyLife' project. The results presented at the second meeting of the steering committee with regard to the innovation ideas, the innovation concept and the innovation process are both convincing and promising. We have also succeeded in creating a fantastic team spirit here over the past few months. The team has prepared well for the upcoming project phase, which centres on implementation. From what you have told me, however, I now realize that roll out and implementation in the organization will confront us with a number of challenges.

As already indicated, I would like to accept your offer of further project support by Sombrero Strategy Consulting in the next phase.

Assignment 11: Preparation of a balanced scorecard for the new strategy. Our discussions have shown that a performance measurement system will be a key success factor for managing our new strategy. We would like to ask you to prepare a balanced scorecard for monitoring the implementation of our new strategy. For a short presentation to our management please prepare a brief list of factors that are essential for the successful implementation of a balanced scorecard in our company.

Assignment 12: Risk management system. From an entrepreneurial perspective we should also look at the risks that could arise from the new strategy. Could your team please deliver a design for an effective and efficient risk management system?

I look forward to continuing our collaboration in the future.

Sincerely yours,
Achim Junick

Dr Achim Junick
Managing Director EasyLife GmbH
EasyLife Group Head Office
Düsseldorf
Germany

Jean-Paul Vutour
From: <jeanpaul.vutour@Sombrero.com>
To: <sian.hang@Sombrero.com>
Sent: Friday 25 February 2011, 11:01
Subject: Consulting project EasyLife

Dear Sian,

First of all, hearty congratulations on successful completion of the initial phase of the EasyLife project. I had no doubt that you and your team would make a success of it!

Before we tackle the next phase, we should as usual have a debriefing session. We can learn a great deal from this external project – you and your team on the one hand and myself from the point of view of the steering committee on the other – and that applies not only to further outside projects but also to internal Sombrero projects.

I would like to hold a meeting with you and your team next Monday (28 February) to take a closer look at the role of innovation managers:

Assignment 13: Lessons learned: To be a driver of innovation strategy means.../does not mean...

I wish you a very pleasant, and for you no doubt relaxing, weekend!

Jean-Paul

PS: When the meeting is over we can talk about the incentive promised to you and the team in connection with the first phase of the project, which has now been completed.

Jean Paul Vutour
Director Sombrero Strategy Consulting (SSC)
St.-Martin-Strasse 76
81541 München

References and
Further Reading

Ambrosini, V, Johnson, G and Scholes, K (1998) *Exploring Techniques of Analysis and Evaluation in Strategic Management*, Prentice Hall Europe / Pearson Education, Harlow

Ansoff, I (1984) *Implanting Strategic Management*, Prentice Hall, Englewood Cliffs, New Jersey

Baum, H G, Coenenberg, A G and Guenther, T (1999) *Strategisches Controlling*, Schäffer-Poeschel, Stuttgart

Coenenberg, A G, Salfeld, R (2003) *Wertorientierte Unternehmensführung*, Schäffer-Poeschel, Stuttgart

Copeland, T, Koller, T and Murrin, J (2000) *Valuation – Measuring and managing the value of companies*, John Wiley and Sons, New York

Dörner, D (1989) *Die Logik des Misslingens*, Rowohlt, Reinbeck, Hamburg

Faulkner, D and Bowman, C (1995) *The Essence of Competitive Strategy*, Pearson Education / Prentice Hall, Harlow

Fink, A, Schlake, O and Siebe, A (2001) *Erfolg durch Szenario – Management. Prinzip und Werkzeuge der strategischen Vorausschau*, Campus, Frankfurt

Geschka, H, Hammer, R (1997) *Die Szenario-Technik in der strategischen Unternehmensplanung*, p. 464–489 in Hahn, D and Taylor, B (Hrsg) (1999) *Strategische Unternehmensplanung – Strategische Unternehmens-führung*, Physika, Heidelberg

Gomez, P and Probst, G J B (1991) *Vernetztes Denken – Ganzheitliches Führen in der Praxis*, Gabler, Wiesbaden

Grosse-Oetringhaus, W F (1996) *Strategische Identität – Orientierung im Wandel – Ganzheitliche Transformation zu Spitzenleistungen*, Springer, Berlin

Hahn, D (1999) Zweck und Entwicklung der Portfolio-Konzepte in der strategischen Unternehmensplanung, in: *Hahn, D and Taylor, B (1999) Strategische Unternehmensplanung – Strategische Unternehmensführung*, Physica, Heidelberg

Hahn, D and Bleicher, K (1999) Organisationsplanung als Gegenstand der strategischen Planung, in: Hahn, D and Taylor, B (1999) *Strategische Unternehmensplanung – Strategische Unternehmensführung, 8. Auflage*, Physica, Heidelberg

Hahn, D and Taylor, B (Hrsg) (1999) *Strategische Unternehmensplanung – Strategische Unternehmensführung*, Physica, Heidelberg

Hahn, D and Willers, H G (1999) Unternehmensplanung und Führungskräftevergütung, in: Hahn, D and Taylor, B (1999) *Strategische Unternehmensplanung – Strategische Unternehmensführung*, Physica, Heidelberg

Hamel, G and Prahalad, C K (1990) The core competence of the corporation, *Harvard Business Review*, May/June

Hax, A C, Wilde II, D L (2001) *The Delta Project – discovering new sources of profitability in a networked economy*, Palgrave, Houndmills

Hinterhuber, H H (1997) *Strategische Unternehmensführung – II. Strategisches Handeln*, Erich Schmidt, Berlin

Johnson, G and Scholes, K (2002) *Exploring Corporate Strategy*, Prentice Hall, Hemel Hempstead

Kaplan, R S and Norton, D P (1996) *The Balanced Scorecard – Translating strategy into action*, Harvard Business School, Boston

Kim, W C and Mauborgne, R (2005) *Blue Ocean Strategy – How to create uncontested market space and make the competition irrelevant*, McGraw Hill, Boston

Kohlöffel, K. M. (2000): *Strategisches Management – Alle Chancen nutzen – Neue Geschäfte erschlieáen*, Hanser, München

Kotler, P (2003) *Marketing Management* 11th ed., Prentice Hall, New Jersey

Mintzberg, H. (1999) *Strategy Safari – eine Reise durch die Wildnis des strategischen Managements*, Redline Wirtschaft, Heidelberg

Porter, M E (1983) *Competitive Strategy – Techniques for analyzing industries and competitors*, Free Press, New York

Porter, M E (1996) *Wettbewerbsvorteile: Spitzenleistungen erreichen und behaupte*, Campus, Frankfurt

Porter, M E (1997) *Wettbewerbsstrategie: Methoden zur Analyse von Branchen und Konkurrenten*, Campus, Frankfurt

Probst, G, Raub, S and Romhardt, K (1999) *Wissen managen*, Gabler, Wiesbaden

Rappaport, A (1986) *Creating Shareholder Value – A guide for managers and investors*, Simon & Schuster, New York / London

Reuter, M P (2007) *Implementierung wertorientierter Unternehmensführung*, Universität Ulm, Ulm

Reutner, F (1995) *Die Strategie-Tagung – Strategische Ziele systematisch erarbeiten und Maánahmen festlegen*, Gabler, Wiesbaden

Schulze, W (2003) *Methoden der Unternehmensbewertung – Gemeinsamkeiten, Unterschiede, Perspektiven*, IDW-Verlag, Düsseldorf

Stewart, G B (1991) *The Quest for Value: The EVA management guide*, Harper Collins, New York

Sun Tzu (1997) *Wahrhaft siegt, wer nicht kämpft: die Kunst der richtigen Strategie*, Freiburg

Thiele, M (1997) *Kernkompetenzorientierte Unternehmensstrukturen – Ansätze zur Neugestaltung von Geschäftsbereichsorganisationen*, Gabler, Wiesbaden

Vester, F (2002) *Die Kunst, vernetzt zu denken*, Deutscher Taschenbuch Verlag, München

Wittmann, R G, Reuter, M P, Magerl, R (2007) *Unternehmensstrategie und Business Plan*, Redline Wirtschaft, Heidelberg

Wolf, K and Runzheimer, B (2003) *Risikomanagement und KonTraG – Konzeption und Implementierung*, Gabler, Wiesbaden

Zur Bonsen, M (1995) *Führen mit Visionen: der Weg zum ganzheitlichen Management*, Gabler, Wiesbaden

Index